Editor-in-Chief and Founder:
    Lyndon H. LaRouche, Jr.
Editorial Board: *Lyndon H. LaRouche, Jr. , Helga
    Zepp-LaRouche, Paul Gallagher, Tony Papert,
    Gerald Rose, Dennis Small, Jeffrey Steinberg,
    William Wertz*
Co-Editors: *Paul Gallagher, Tony Papert*
Managing Editor: *Nancy Spannaus*
Technology: *Marsha Freeman*
Books: *Katherine Notley*
Ebooks: *Richard Burden*
Graphics: *Alan Yue*
Photos: *Stuart Lewis*
Circulation Manager: *Stanley Ezrol*

INTELLIGENCE DIRECTORS
Counterintelligence: *Jeffrey Steinberg, Michele
    Steinberg*
Economics: *John Hoefle, Marcia Merry Baker,
    Paul Gallagher*
History: *Anton Chaitkin*
Ibero-America: *Dennis Small*
Russia and Eastern Europe: *Rachel Douglas*
United States: *Debra Freeman*

INTERNATIONAL BUREAUS
Bogotá: *Miriam Redondo*
Berlin: *Rainer Apel*
Copenhagen: *Tom Gillesberg*
Houston: *Harley Schlanger*
Lima: *Sara Madueño*
Melbourne: *Robert Barwick*
Mexico City: *Gerardo Castilleja Chávez*
New Delhi: *Ramtanu Maitra*
Paris: *Christine Bierre*
Stockholm: *Ulf Sandmark*
United Nations, N.Y.C.: *Leni Rubinstein*
Washington, D.C.: *William Jones*
Wiesbaden: *Göran Haglund*

ON THE WEB
e-mail: eirns@larouchepub.com
www.larouchepub.com
www.executiveintelligencereview.com
www.larouchepub.com/eiw
Webmaster: *John Sigerson*
Assistant Webmaster: *George Hollis*
Editor, Arabic-language edition: *Hussein Askary*

EIR (ISSN 0273-6314) *is published weekly
(50 issues), by EIR News Service, Inc.,
P.O. Box 17390, Washington, D.C. 20041-0390.
(703) 777-9451*

European Headquarters: E.I.R. GmbH, Postfach
Bahnstrasse 9a, D-65205, Wiesbaden, Germany
Tel: 49-611-73650
Homepage: http://www.eirna.com
e-mail: eirna@eirna.com
Director: Georg Neudecker

Montreal, Canada: 514-461-1557

Denmark: EIR - Danmark, Sankt Knuds Vej 11,
basement left, DK-1903 Frederiksberg, Denmark.
Tel.: +45 35 43 60 40, Fax: +45 35 43 87 57. e-mail:
eirdk@hotmail.com.

Mexico City: EIR, Sor Juana Inés de la Cruz 242-2
Col. Agricultura C.P. 11360
Delegación M. Hidalgo, México D.F.
Tel. (5525) 5318-2301
eirmexico@gmail.com

Canada Post Publication Sales Agreement
#40683579

Postmaster: Send all address changes to *EIR*, P.O.
Box 17390, Washington, D.C. 20041-0390.

Signed articles in *EIR* represent the views of the
authors, and not necessarily those of the Editorial
Board.

Start from Roosevelt's Overall Conception

LaRouche Replies to Questions From Russian Journalist

Below are Lyndon H. LaRouche's replies to questions posed by a Russian journalist on Sept. 20, regarding four subject areas.

Question 1: Europe faces a huge refugee crisis nowadays. To what extent can it harm the EU economy? Is the integration of the European Union now under a real threat?

LaRouche: The prospective subject of a "huge refugees crisis" is not actually a presently required consideration. It nonetheless represents a matter of presently deadly risks on nothing less than a global scale: a presently still profound risk which must be soon defeated. In essential principle, it would be defeated, were the present United States of America freed from the legacy of the presently traditional British Empire's admittedly still menacing grip on the United States of America.

There have been a crucially important minority of useful leaders of the United States of America, despite the relatively greater extent of wretches who have actually occupied that office. Admittedly, the present risk remains truly great; but, there is no present alternative, excepting the presently hopeful options for a now prevailing great peace.

Question 2: Europe bears the losses because of its sanction policy against Russia. Do you think the EU should revise this policy, taking into account the situation with refugees?

LaRouche: Recently, there have been two notable changes in certain European sectors, which have been, most notably the converging efforts, in effect, between Germany and leading elements within the bounds of Eurasia, and, implicitly, others. The presently strenuous conditions affecting the economies of Russia and its relevant neighbors can, and must be efficiently addressed, however difficult during the relatively short term.

Question 3: Speaking of the ruble's weakening, what do you think are the roots of it? Does the West want to weaken the Russian economy by imposing new sanctions?

LaRouche: Of course, there is a plentiful supply of those wishing to "weaken the Russian economy." Soon, the trans-Atlantic economic breakdown crisis will be pushed into a sundry set of general breakdown economic crises of their own. Wall Street, now, for example.

Question 4: How do you think the Russian economy can cope with this crisis and avoid a negative impact from Western policy towards Russia?

LaRouche: For the case of the United States, in particular, the United Nations, considered as a whole, during the term of the present weeks, now presents the generality of the trans-Atlantic, Eurasian and related regions. I explain.

The general conditions of the regions throughout the nations of our planet, and, now, implicitly beyond, are already, presently, bringing about the generally systemic, immediate collapse of what has been long the systemic crisis of the origins of the economies of both the British Empire and its roots. The range of that particular region of World History, since the crushing of the principal political powers of the Renaissance, is now menaced by the emergence of a new Renaissance, a Renaissance which rejects all that the British Empire and its lackeys represent. The world at large is presently located within the verge of the end of the existence of the legacy of the British Empire and its particular roots.

On this account, in particular, everything which has been a sort of victim of the British Empire, is presently doomed to oblivion. This includes, in particular, the expressions of the British system's legacy, that same legacy which was resurrected afresh by evil Bertrand Russell's system of world economy. That legacy which has been continued under the systemic influence of the so-called Twentieth Century system, has now reached a condition of a general, global demise of the presently doomed order of "money system" premised upon products of the British Empire and its roots.

What the Monetary System Actually Means

Simply, for example: The U.S. "Wall Street" system, and its likenesses, are now in the actual termination of any of their continued qualities of existence. I mean the very principle of "monetary systems, as such." What must replace that system, and all its ordinary licences, is the creative powers associated with the principle of the rising power of efficiently practiced human creativity.

Take, for example, the scientific principles coincident with Johannes Kepler's discovery of the notion of a Solar System, or the greater instrument, the galactic system.

⣿⣿EIR Contents

www.larouchepub.com Volume 42, Number 38, September 25, 2015

**Cover
This Week**

*President
Franklin
Roosevelt giving
a fireside chat on
Columbus Day
1942*

Start from Franklin Roosevelt's Overall Concept

by Dave Christie, LaRouche PAC Policy Committee

Wall Street is totally bankrupt, and it's coming down very fast now. The only solutions are preemptive ones that start from the re-installation of Franklin Roosevelt's Glass-Steagall law. *But*, if you don't present the overall solution as starting from the overall concept of Franklin Roosevelt's total, overall solution, and working down from there,—then you'll just wind up with chaos.

On a closely related question: Not only do we have to completely wipe out Wall Street, and have the government step in. We also have to establish real valuations, as against the current, and false, money-valuations. Then, we proceed from there, through the first difficult steps of reconstruction, and onwards into a self-sustaining and self-accelerating physical-economic recovery, and into a new era for mankind.

Wall Street is about to blow sky-high. Now we have to go back, in effect, to the beginning of the Twentieth Century, before the imposition of the money system, the system which was premised first of all on the great crime of President William McKinley's 1901 assassination. By now, we have reached the point under this money system, where there is no way whatsoever to measure true, intrinsic values. Now, Franklin Roosevelt's entire

Franklin Delano Roosevelt (1882-1945), 32nd President of the United States

concept, as a totality, must be brought into play to have any hope of a solution.

At the same time, Russia has taken the initiative in Syria, and is pushing through a solution to the catastrophe Obama has inflicted on that country, and more generally. More and more, the whole world supports what Putin is doing there,—including many forces in the U.S. Absent this Russian initiative, Syria and Iraq would fail totally. Indeed, all of Obama's policies can produce nothing but failure. His influence must be totally blocked; unless Obama is induced to back down, he will destroy everything. Obama is an ugly loser. Nothing must be done to encourage Obama; everything must be done to support Putin's leadership. Obama can only be allowed, at most, to make token gestures with no effect.

Look: The major European countries have turned against Obama's policy. Russia is leading the world against Obama's policy. Therefore, there's no need for Obama's approval. When you have Europe and Russia, there's no need for Obama's OK; he's almost stymied. Now, what we need is the 25th Amendment to finish off his baleful influence altogether.

—LaRouche PAC statement,
September 17, 2015

Sept. 22—The world will soon gather in Manhattan for the last week of September at the United Nations General Assembly. Obama will speak on September 28th, one month before the Seventieth Anniversary of the ratification of the United Nations Charter in October of 1945. However, the world will now no longer simply gather to listen to Obama's diktat, issued forth from his masters within the British Empire. Instead, the world will gather together as a new paradigm is being consolidated, led by the BRICS process, which has the very real potential to unleash a Renaissance for all of mankind, in the face of the crumbling edifice of the British Empire. As Lyndon LaRouche recently stated, the evil Bertrand Russell's system of world economy is now doomed.

In that light, I recently had the opportunity to discuss the importance of Franklin Roosevelt with Phil Rubinstein, a long-time leader within the international movement of Lyndon LaRouche. The article that follows will contain excerpts from that discussion on the importance of understanding what Franklin Roosevelt did to combat the world outlook of Bertrand Russell.

Rubinstein began the discussion by elaborating on Franklin Roosevelt's intent to dismantle the British Empire. Roosevelt's leadership was unique in the Twentieth Century, and from the very beginning he moved to crush Wall Street, and show the American people its rot and corruption.

FDR versus Wall Street

Rubinstein: In reflecting on the destruction of the Twentieth Century, it's clear that Franklin Roosevelt really represents the only leadership, really the only President of the United States, to successfully combat, up to a point, the destruction of culture, the destruction of civilization through the wars that have typified the Twentieth Century, and have continued into the Twenty-First Century in an even worse way. In particular, he took on the British Empire, which had become, in fact, an "empire of the mind."

There are a number of things you could touch upon that created the situation into which FDR came, concerning the Great Depression, and the build-up to World War II, which was in many ways a continuation of World War I. But the fact is, he was unique in

Ferdinand Pecora, Chief Counsel to the U.S. Senate Committee on Banking and Currency during its investigation of Wall Street under Franklin Roosevelt.

his leadership. Of course, we've had other leaders who weren't terrible, but in many ways they were unable to act, or were limited in their actions. Kennedy, of course, had his life and presidency cut short. Others, perhaps, such as Eisenhower, were constrained in terms of their own limitations—there were decent Presidents, but no one really led the United States consistently against the British rule and essentially saved the United States; saved civilization in fact.

Since FDR's death, the British Empire has had a nearly seamless cultural takeover of the United States, and the transatlantic world in general, that now brings us to the final phase of collapse—which, of course, brings the threat of war.

The point we must consider today, is that we cannot simply try to repeat what FDR did; that's not possible. We're in a different period, and if anything, the situation we face today is far worse. But we can understand the principle that FDR stood for, and that he fought successfully for, which allowed us to defeat fascism, and had us on the road to something totally different concerning his vision of the United Nations as a platform for the development of relations among nations—a kind of orientation of mankind toward common economic development. But he didn't live to see that through, and his successors weren't up to the task, so we're now faced with the threat of extinction.

Roosevelt was very clear. He said we didn't need Wall Street; we'd be better off without it. From day one, he took on Wall Street—really from before day one, as New York Governor, and then in his campaign for the Presidency—he said that the government represents the interests of the population, and that people have priority over Wall Street, and in fact, we didn't need Wall Street, since it was their speculative financial junk that destroyed a good part of the world in the 1920s, and into the Great Depression. And that is an important message for many Americans who are simply terrified of Wall Street.

The Pecora Commission

Rubinstein went on to discuss the importance of Ferdinand Pecora, and his commission that sent Wall Street criminals to jail. This laid the groundwork for the ensuing passage of Glass-Steagall, after the American people saw the abuses they endured under these "high priests of the Temple of Finance." This is an especially important message for all those Americans today, and their political leaders, who accept the idea that Wall Street is too-big-to-fail, and too-big-to-jail.

Rubinstein: What is important to remember is that there was a predecessor to the Pecora Commission—there was already an investigation of Wall Street—but it did nothing; it failed completely. The reason, of course, had to do with the fact that Hoover was a Wall Street backer, and the people who were appointed had no intention of following through and prosecuting Wall Street, to make it clear that Wall Street was the problem—the likes of J.P. Morgan, William Mitchell of National City, and so forth. Pecora was then brought in, and then Roosevelt was elected, which gave Pecora the go-ahead to fully prosecute Wall Street; and he did.

These guys were convicted, and they served terms—they were humiliated. It was clear that they were the problem, that Roosevelt was not going to put up with them, and Pecora had the courage to go after them. Had it not been for Roosevelt, we would have seen the same gutless cowardice we see today.

The jailing of Mitchell, and the humiliation of Morgan, is a total contrast to the *carte blanche* that Wall Street has been given over the recent years, explicitly by the Obama-Holder combine, which said that Wall Street rules, and is more important than the rest of the nation. They're too-big-to-fail; they're too big to prosecute.

But that was not Roosevelt's view, as he famously said in his inauguration that we would chase the money changers out of the temple; but most especially, he focused over and over again, on the reality that the speculative financial activities of Wall Street were not in the interest of the nation. He basically took the Pecora Commission—as he took the Reconstruction Finance Corporation, as he took the Federal Reserve,—and he forced them, and he used them, not just to circumvent Wall Street, but to replace Wall Street, and to replace a monetarist system, forcing these institutions into subservience of the nation.

National Archive

From Day One of his Presidency, FDR set out to rebuild and save the nation. Here, CCC workers grading a rural road ca. 1935.

FDR versus the British Empire

For these actions, Franklin Roosevelt was called a "traitor to his class." This could be no more clearly stated in his first inaugural address, when he said that the economic situation and the unemployment caused by Wall Street, must be treated as "we would treat the emergency of war," and spoke of "broad executive power to wage war against this emergency, as great as the power given to me if we were in fact invaded by a foreign foe." Rubinstein elaborated further on his wartime mobilization, and showed that Roosevelt was very clear on who the enemy was—the British Empire.

Rubinstein: It's important to see that this is Roosevelt from day one of his Administration, all the way through the 1930s, where he basically set the conditions for saving U.S. industry, saving U.S. agriculture, saving the labor force through the Works Progress Administration, the Civilian Conservation Corps, and mobilizing credit through the Reconstruction Finance Corporation. He set the conditions under which we basically created the greatest industrial economic machine in human history, adding to it certain rapid scientific development.

At the same time, he opposed Wall Street and their policies from day one, emphatically including his conflicts with Winston Churchill over the British Empire, and through his Bretton Woods Conference, where Roosevelt and his delegation attacked the idea of the imperial preferences in trade in the Commonwealth, as well as in his call for the independence of India.

So he was an enemy of the British Empire and monetarism from the beginning to the end; it was a unifying characteristic of his entire Presidency—fair trade, not free trade; the Good Neighbor Policy; his conception of the United Nations. These are all part of his anti-monetarist, anti-empire Presidency. And, indeed, he was the most advanced representative of the American System.

Battle for the Mind

As Lyndon LaRouche has stressed in the recent period, it was after the British directed assassination of President William McKinley in 1901 that the monetarist system was ushered in. In addition to identifying Bertrand Russell as "the most evil man of the Twentieth Century," LaRouche has also pointed to Russell as the font of intellectual garbage that has become the basis for that monetarist system. It is immoral, precisely because it systematically denies the future, and the development of creativity, which is the basis for the productive power of our labor force. With no future conception, any system of society and economy will be relegated to the stagnant swamp of deductive systems. Rubinstein has written articles discussing the role of Russell. He also discussed his grasp of what Franklin Roosevelt did to counter this world outlook.

Rubinstein: I think this is an important issue to review in terms of our efforts to educate and organize people, as we create a Renaissance. You can also say that Roosevelt is one of the remaining products of the Renaissance which created the American Revolution, which largely has been put into the background by the British Empire.

The example to use here is Bertrand Russell, and to a degree, David Hilbert—what is it that they did? I think it's interesting. It is roughly about 1900 when Hilbert put forward the idea of axiomatizing physics. Russell was already working on this project; he was attacking Riemann and Leibniz, but the real point was to attack the human mind, the creativity of the human mind. This is particularly reflected in the human mind's ability to act on the future, to create a future which otherwise would not come into existence.

Any system, any economic system, that is rooted in a given set of scientific principles that are utilized in the technology, that's rooted in a given sense of traditional culture, is going to run up against its limits—the limits of the existing science and technology, the limits of the traditional culture. You won't have a population that's capable of creating or acting or thinking of acting on the future, but instead, one which simply believes that its task is to repeat the past, and that we will not have the

British Empire representative Bertrand Russell, shown here lecturing in 1939 at the University of California, Los Angeles, laid out the "philosophy" of Wall Street.

capability to make the necessary scientific breakthroughs which represent discovery of principles otherwise unknown at the time.

This discovery of principle is the basis for the development of human activity and human economy. Therefore, the core of human activity is creativity, expressed in being able to create a future existence that goes into future generations, not just the next generation, but, in a certain sense, you're preparing future generations, so that they themselves think in terms of the future. So you establish creative development as the core of value, which is expressed in the productivity of labor.

Russell, along with Hilbert and some of these others, but Russell, in particular, says that truth can be axiomatized. They created formal system and a set of axioms, all modelled on Euclid—exactly what Euclid and Aristotle did, even with the prior knowledge of the Greek renaissance—to attempt to create a formal system that would then be the limit of knowledge.

Russell's 'Empire of the Mind'

At this point in the discussion, I raised the fact that both Russell and Hilbert were involved in launching the International Congress for the Unity of Sciences in 1935, during the beginning of FDR's Presidency. This was an outgrowth of the Ernst Mach Society. Ernst Mach was famous for his "suspicion of anything metaphysical," and of course, what could be further beyond the senses than the future itself? These were the figures behind statistics, which is the foundation of the thinking (or non-thinking) of Wall Street, where there is no sense of the future, just gambling and playing the markets. Einstein made a very clear attack on this crowd when he said, "God does not play dice."

Rubinstein: Exactly. Russell attempted to produce an axiomatic system, based on the logic of arithmetic. But it wasn't just that; because their view was that all scientific measurement (effectively, it was called real numbers, and so forth), could be axiomatized. And therefore if you axiomatized arithmetic, you essentially formalized the entirety of scientific knowledge.

You might accidentally find yourself running into some new capability that you can incorporate as a new axiom—but essentially truth, the certainty of truth, is embodied in logical deduction from a given axiomatic system, which in this case an axiomatic system that was meant to be the mathematical model of everything. This is absolutely the basis of information theory; it's the whole model that a lot of people have experienced as deductive and inductive science. You simply catalogue experiences, you get the measurements of those experiences, you make a generalization, and then you deduce some prediction from it.

Now, nowhere in this is there a creation of a new idea; or really, what's more important, a new principle—a universal principle, like electromagnetism, like what Kepler does with his development of the solar system. Universal principles are what give you reality.

One of the most immoral things about Russell—and this is what Roosevelt fought—is the idea that you can't create the future; which means that you have no moral responsibility. It's immoral if human beings cannot use the creative capabilities to act jointly to bring a future that's required into existence, and find the path and new principle that will allow you to do it. The point is that they've taken the mind and the morality out of humanity. Without the ability to create the future, all you can do is repeat the past. And if your standard of truth is formal deduction, then there is no content; all you're doing is formally rearranging symbols and drawing out something that's already there, at best.

Now the thing to realize is that the entirety of Wall Street is based on this. What's free trade? What's the free market? It's to not think; cognition is actually not only unnecessary, but a bad intrusion into reality—the human mind is somehow an external feature that shouldn't be involved. You should act on your desires, your fears, which can thereby be used to price financial instruments.

How do we price them? We make certain kinds of bets on what people are willing to pay financially for certain pleasures and to avoid certain pains. Ultimately, then, the whole issue is the growth of monetary value. You have money making money. This is all based on mathematical models, what are called algorithms,— mechanical, deductive systems, which are largely based on statistical preferences. And that's why you have rocket scientists on Wall Street today.

This was done on a lower level in the 1920s, although the principle was the same. This is what Roosevelt was fighting. People were betting on the value of stocks; they were betting on the value of futures and indexes; and this grew into the 1950s, '60s and '70s and into what we now call derivatives—you can bet on what is going to be the Dow Jones index 30 days from now. So you have trillions and trillions of dollars in this area, and from a monetarist standpoint, that's value! Roosevelt knew that this had absolutely no value. Of course, today, we have almost the *reductio ad absurdum* of this concept of value.

A Worse Challenge Today

This *reductio ad absurdum* that Rubinstein mentioned, has probably cost the American people far more than the $23 trillion that former TARP Inspector General, Neil Barofsky, cited in his Congressional testimony as the potential cost of the Federal bailouts after 2007-08. These bailouts are symptomatic of the disease of Wall Street, and are a part of the economic crisis, but they are not the only part. In addition to the moral and intellectual rot created by Russell, there is the destruction of the labor force, which makes the recovery far more difficult today than in Roosevelt's time. Rubinstein went on to discuss this matter.

Rubinstein: You have to realize that at that time, 25 percent, or more, of the American population was still on farms. Today, it's 1-2 percent. Then, these farms still had a certain productive capability, so people could go back to their farms. Many people had relatives who were on farms. It is also the case that the U.S. was only a dozen or so years from the World War I build-up, so a great deal of the industry had not been degraded over a twenty, thirty, almost a forty-year period of degradation

An abandoned blast furnce in Pittsburgh, Pennsylvania.

rustwire.com

of the entire manufacturing facility, as it has been today.

New economic sectors were on the rise, such as the beginning of airplane production, whatever its limitations. We're in a situation now where we've lost a good deal of our aerospace sector. We've lost our automobile industry; it virtually shut down in the first decade of this century. LaRouche was engaged in a major effort to save the auto industry because of its machine tool capability—we've lost all of that. We've basically given up our space program which was the science driver of the '50s and '60s, and so on and so forth.

So we're much worse off. Indeed the economy has virtually minuscule productivity relative to the financial values that are estimated at 1.5-2 quadrillion dollars; my view is that, in principle, it's an infinite amount, because they roll these instruments over, they pile new leverage on top of it, and it just keeps expanding. It has no connection to any real production.

The global Transatlantic system that has been hegemonic up to the present, is dead. You see this in Europe; you see this in Southern Europe; you see it in the United States—in the healthcare, in the education; this system is fundamentally a dead system. And we're at the point where people have to recognize that they don't need Wall Street; and that what they think they are worried about, losing their nest egg, is complete folly—they've lost it already. We saw that in 2007-2008.

We're seeing it again. As soon as people get to the point where they have to use their so-called monetary value in the stock market or other financial investments, it's not there! It doesn't exist, and it won't exist. And this is a tough one—a monetarist system means that you can build value on nothing; and that's exactly what they have done.

The 1900 Turning Point

Rubinstein returned to the assassination of McKinley, and the attempt by Russell and Hilbert to create the "empire of the mind" to crush the emerging political economy known as the American System of Hamilton and Lincoln, that was blossoming throughout the world, especially in Eurasia.

Rubinstein: I think that the 1900s is not just Russell and Hilbert. Russell is an extremely important figure in this, because he really legitimizes the entirely anti-scientific insane economic outlook, but it really is an economic policy. Most of economic policy of the Twentieth Century roots itself in this kind of mathematical model—game theory and so forth.

Now, at the same time, what is this? This is the British Empire. Remember, Russell and his whole family was part of the British Aristocracy. Even more than that, Russell took it upon himself to play the leading role in the epistemological domination of this anti-human, anti-creative outlook and conception of human activity, which essentially reduced human beings to an animal or a machine. This is why you have so much confusion, increasingly in the Twentieth Century: "What are we. . are we merely machines, do we know better than an animal?" This is all Russell.

But, the thing to keep in mind is that this is all part of the effort to extend the existence of the British Empire, to extend its reach. The British Empire had already come to an internal collapse at the end of the Nineteenth Century. Across the globe, you had forces moving in the direction of industrial development modelled on the United States; you had it in Russia; you had it in Germany under Bismarck who was removed in 1890; you had some figures of this sort in France; you had it in China under Sun Yat Sen.

An artist's rendition of Teddy Roosevelt's charge up San Juan Hill in the Spanish-American War.

Prince Albert, who became Edward VII, took upon himself the task of extending the reach of the British Empire. A big part of this led into World War I. A big part of this was the United States rolling back, effectively, the American Revolution; you had the Confederacy, and the resurrection of the Confederacy. But this culminated in the assassination of McKinley, who was the last representative of some of the better features—Lincoln, Grant, and others of the Nineteenth-century American System.

McKinley was assassinated through British networks, and what came in? Teddy Roosevelt. Now, Teddy Roosevelt viewed the United States as part of the English-speaking British Empire. For the first time, whatever all the flaws were—you had animals like Jackson, killing Indians and pro-slavery, and so on; you had some Wall Street figures like Van Buren, and you had confederates—but it's with Teddy Roosevelt that you have the idea that the United States is really part of the British Empire.

You know, famously, his uncle on his mother's side was a figure within Confederate intelligence, his mother was an active Confederate supporter, and he was a supporter of the British Imperial outlook. This was his claim to fame,—as in San Juan Hill and the whole story. He remained a dominant figure beyond his Presidency into the 1910s, where he was big advocate of supporting the British in the World War I.

Then we had Woodrow Wilson, who followed Teddy Roosevelt. Wilson was an apologist for the Confederacy. Members of his family were hardcore Confederate activists, his history of the United States was an apology for the Confederacy, and he himself was a proponent of the British Imperial outlook. He rooted himself in the outlook of some of the leading late Eighteenth Century British thinkers, and he of course brought in the Ku Klux Klan, and infamously screened "The Birth of a Nation," which was a Confederate propaganda film, at the White House.

What you got then,—and it's often taken as a coherent series of events,—was the FBI, the Federal Reserve, and Wilson the Confederate. This was all one process of undermining us, and really, and drawing the United States, through Wall Street, through the hegemony of Wall Street, into an extended British Empire. And the British have thought this way: the extension of the Empire into the Commonwealth.

The truth of the matter is, through most of the Twentieth Century, other than the period of Roosevelt himself (FDR), this has been dominant. And by the 1970s, it had essentially taken over. You had Truman, who was a worshipper of Winston Churchill, and Churchill was an Empire man. The only thing I can say is that Churchill was less sophisticated than Russell. Russell was really rooted in the idea of the Empire, and had little or no loyalty to a place, even Britain. Churchill was a British Empire man, and that clash came out during World War II. Russell supported the Nazis until 1940.

FDR versus Churchill

Franklin Roosevelt had numerous brawls with Winston Churchill about the nature of man. Roosevelt's son, Elliott, wrote a book called "As He Saw It," which gave an intimate picture of this fight, perhaps best encapsulated in an exchange where Roosevelt was discussing the need for development of poorer nations. Roosevelt referenced India, the Jewel of the British Crown, and caught the ire of Churchill, to which Roosevelt responded, "I can't believe that we can fight a war against fascist slavery, and at the same time not work to free people all over the world from a backward colonial policy."

Roosevelt's passionate fight against empire was at

the core of his idea behind the United Nations and all of the related institutions that would later come out of the Bretton Woods Conference. Those institutions, such as the World Bank and the International Monetary Fund, have obviously become instruments of the British Empire today. However, the upcoming UN General Assembly can be an opportunity to actually carry out the intention of Roosevelt, which, in part, is being carried forward with the BRICS process.

Rubinstein: I think this was Roosevelt from day one, until the day he died in the presidency. He was asked soon before he died—the British knew he was going to die. He had polio, and other severe medical problems that were known to the British, and I think they outlasted him. They put tremendous pressure on him in the 1944 Convention to get rid of Wallace as his Vice-Presidential candidate, and we ended up with Truman; Roosevelt had simply hoped to live through his fourth term.

Soon before this occurred, when he got back from Yalta, or maybe earlier, he was asked what he wanted to do after the war,—to which he responded that he would not have minded becoming the Secretary General of the United Nations. Now, the basic idea that he had was to use the United Nations as a means of working through the necessary development for the colonial world. His view was that we had to end the idea of colonies. Our whole relationship to countries like Vietnam, Indonesia, Iran, Ghana, what became the Non-Aligned Movement —you could go through a whole list—was completely different under Roosevelt. His intention was to liberate these countries and develop them, starting with massive infrastructure projects: rail, water management, etc. He was famous as an expert in geography, and a lot of this was what allowed him to create a vision of development, infrastructural development, which would be a platform to improve these economies, and the United Nations would be a platform for discussing this and bringing new nations into existence.

Now, that was brought to Bretton Woods. As I said, one of the big points was the idea of a universal currency by Keynes. But the big point was they were not going to give up the imperial preferences. What did that

One of FDR's clashes with Churchill was over FDR's vision for post-war institutions such as the United Nations. Here, the two are shown aboard the USS Quincy prior to the Yalta conference with Stalin in 1945.

mean? Free Trade did not apply to the Commonwealth, so that, for example, the different colonies, or former colonies that were members of the Commonwealth, had to buy preferentially, British-produced goods, or goods within the Empire. So, the Free Trade rules and constraints would not apply to the Commonwealth and the colonies. This was rejected by Roosevelt's representative Harry Dexter White. Of course, this was not the free trade that people talk about today. Now, it means that everyone has to succumb to the markets,—versus what Roosevelt called "fair trade," where developing countries would be able to protect their development of industries and agriculture, and so forth.

Today, this is now being brought forward by China, India, with the collaboration with Russia, South Africa, Brazil, as a new development, or what Xi Jinping and the Chinese call a "win-win" strategy; this is what Putin has identified himself with increasingly.

Of course, the other aspect of this, that goes to the Putin side of this, is that Roosevelt, like Eisenhower, like MacArthur, like many of the military men, recognized, that with the sheer destructive power, represented in WWII, almost by itself,—let alone with the addition of the atomic weapons used on Hiroshima and Nagasaki,—they recognized that general warfare, of the type we saw in World War I and World War II, or the threat of that kind of warfare, was a threat to the existence of the human species. Roosevelt knew it, and therefore he saw the United Nations as a place where these kinds of problems could be worked out.

Compare that to the British view, which used the conflicts to keep these nations at bay and undeveloped. And this was immediately seen in the Korean War, in the way in which nations were divided, and in the whole way in which the Soviets were treated. You see it up to this day. Roosevelt wasn't a believer in Communism, nor did he think that the Soviets were simply to be trusted,—he simply recognized that you had to develop a relationship with the Soviet Union, and he saw that he had the same problem with the British Empire, only worse.

His view was that we had to have the United Nations, we had to bring in the Soviets, on an equal basis. And of course, very interestingly, Roosevelt wanted China in the Big Four. You had the Big Three,—the United States, Great Britain, and the Soviet Union,— and he insisted on bringing in China, even though of course as a military power, or an economic power, it didn't compare. But he saw China as a great nation, just as he had argued for the independence of India, and that the future of the human species depended on bringing China and India as great nations into the overall dialogue,—and that was his view of the United Nations. Churchill and the British were totally against bringing China in. In effect, the British and their allies in the United States supported Mao.

So this is a totally different picture of the world,— really, you could say, in the American intellectual tradition. This is where you see whatever value there is in the American history of the American System. This is a profound idea,—this is why the best way to look at it, is to look at what Roosevelt represents, versus what Russell represented, what Edward VII represented: an anti-human outlook, which we see in the House of Windsor today in the idea of reducing the population of the world under the green policy. Roosevelt's idea of a green policy was to plant three billion trees, and they changed the weather and ended the dustbowl—by development.

A New Renaissance

Rubinstein then went on to discuss the importance of the cultural development promoted by not only Franklin Roosevelt, but especially the work of his wife, Eleanor.

Rubinstein: It's a funny thing, because in their own way, Lyn and Helga have made the point that the only way to organize now, is from the standpoint of a new renaissance of taking on the frontier problems—like

FDR Library
Civilian Conservation Corp workers planting trees in 1933.

the role of the galaxy in the development of the planet earth, the fundamental issues of science, and culture. I hate to even make that distinction between "science" versus "culture." They are leading in the development of Classical music, using the choruses to create the conditions under which we can produce composers, and the role of various people in keeping that alive.

Roosevelt and his wife Eleanor, even given whatever limitations they may have had, were certainly very keen to the idea that you needed to maintain an orientation to developing culture. Eleanor Roosevelt did extremely important work on the civil rights question. She was a great supporter during the New Deal for the efforts of the government to finance music, drama, and the plastic arts. Some of it may not have been up to the level of classical culture, but, frankly, some of it showed some potential and some promise. There is much to be said about the fact that one of the problems Roosevelt had was with the southern Democrats, as they shut down much of the efforts in the arts, but I think both Franklin and Eleanor Roosevelt at least had a sense of this,—and of course, Eleanor was completely dedicated to working with African-American artists,—Marian Anderson, Paul Robeson and others,—and she herself was persecuted by the same forces in the government that went after civil rights leaders.

So you have to really look at that as part of the package. I think it's important to see how singular this all was, and then of course, in the same vein,—I mean the whole point of the New Deal,—what was the credit policy of the new Deal based on? This is the same economic policy as Lyn's. Lyn has a more developed version. We have to deal with some international problems: a global Glass

Steagall, a financial system that works across international borders in a much more positive way and so forth,—but, let's give Roosevelt his due.

He had the Four Corners, the St. Lawrence Seaway, the Hoover Dam and of course the Grand Coulee, and just one good example is his building of this infrastructure, a lot of which was predicated on spreading electrical power throughout the country. In this case of hydroelectric power, that was the basis for the whole development of the aluminum industry in the Northwest and the expansion of the aerospace industry.

Then you had the TVA, which became a global model. And this was the first and maybe the only case of real industrial development in the southern states, stretching into northern Alabama and even northern Mississippi. And these are the kinds of projects that elevate the population, that give them the basis in education, and they were models for China, for Egypt and others, in the spread of this idea and this kind of activity. The Chinese openly modeled the Three Gorges Dam project on what they saw in the TVA and other such examples.

Then, of course, you have the reality, as Lyn has mentioned himself very recently, that, let's say, the critical moment in his life was the end of WWII. He had served, as 16-17 million Americans had, and Roosevelt died. And Lyn was in a position to discuss with some of the other GIs what the future would bring. They came to him. And Lyn said, "We have to have a devotion to the same principles that Roosevelt represented, and to fight the same fight."

And I think that Lyn and Helga,—Lyn obviously being of the age,—have committed themselves to that. And I think we have uncovered, in a sense, the deeper fight that Roosevelt was involved in, in this battle against the British Empire.

Here we are today. The British Empire is really dead. It cannot support a population. Wall Street is rotten to the core. The City of London is the enemy of the human species. The empire of the mind that they built, not through some conspiracy of brainwashing in some sense of controlling your neural networks, but the empire of the mind typified by Russell, and all of this garbage that's been brought in. It's all dead. It struck me, when Jeb Bush was asked who he would put on the

Smithsonian Institution, National Museum of American History
Eleanor Roosevelt played a major role in arranging contralto Marian Anderson's historic concert at the Lincoln Memorial on April 9, 1939.

ten dollar bill to replace Hamilton, and he said Margaret Thatcher. Now, that's pretty far gone.

Closing Thoughts

Rubinstein: You come back to Lincoln. Given where we are now, and as I said, you have the moves by Putin to try to outflank the efforts to create war in Ukraine, war that could be nuclear, a serious threat of nuclear war. You have the effort to outflank this in the Middle East, but also in relation to the BRICS and China. Our task really is a serious one. We can have a lot of fun with it.

We have to break Americans from this insane commitment to Wall Street, to a monetary outlook on the world, to forgetting that we are human beings, that the value lies in human beings, in elevating the creative powers of human beings, in creating the conditions where more and more human beings are being given the opportunity to activate their creative powers, to extend those powers further into the universe, to carry out a mission, which is to be creative, as we were created to be.

I have no problem in saying that we've evolved to be creative, because creativity is what's built into the universe, and we have to give up the idea we are somehow creatures of money, and we have to give up our ability to think in the marketplace, with some mechanical set of statistical rules. We have to elevate ourselves and elevate our fellow citizens, so they don't degrade themselves to dance to the tune of the moneymakers.

Creating the Harmony of Nations

Here are edited excerpts of Lyndon LaRouche's Dialogue with the Manhattan Project on Sept 19, 2015.

Dennis Speed: On behalf of the LaRouche Political Action Committee, I want to welcome everybody here today. My name is Dennis Speed. We're going to go into our dialogue with Lyndon LaRouche immediately.

As people know, we've now begun the extraordinary session of the United Nations, and Mr. LaRouche has said several things about that session, and about what its implications can be. I want one thing to be clear: Certainly what we want done with respect to that session, is that Barack Obama, the erstwhile President of the United States, be removed through the actions that we intend to take, including as they impact that session, and as that session impacts the United States.

So, Lyn, I want to first invite you, if you want, to give us some opening remarks, and if not, we'll go right to questions, if you would prefer that.

Lyndon LaRouche: *Well, we are now, as you know, on the verge of the participation in Manhattan, and elsewhere, of a very important event, an event which may determine the judgments made to bring about a safe reconstruction of the relations of the planets, and together with those on Earth. And I think that in the course of time, that statement from me will stand up.*

So, why don't we just take it that way, and let's see what the result is in the minds of our people here, gathered today.

Speed: Okay, I like that!

Q: Hi, Lyn. It's A—from New York. I'd like your help regarding,—in this upcoming week now that we're going to rally and intervene in the UN,—this has, as you talked about or referenced, worldwide historical effects, and I'd like for you to help describe that a little bit. But more specifically, I'm working through your paper on global warming and population control, and in the process of looking to work through this with others, be it through phone calls, or discussions. So I'd like your help on that, because Obama is a focus, a center point, of this operation that we need to snap, and so with that in mind, give us a hand here.

LaRouche: Well, I would say that everything about Obama is dissonant, and therefore it has no real human resonance. This is true in terms of the way he speaks, if you listen to him. Listen to him when he makes speeches. You say, this man is a dissonant character.

One of the panels which decorated the singers' gallery in the great Florence cathedral, one of the jewels of the Italian Renaissance.

When he says things, or when he starts to make proposals, the same effect comes in. And the question is, why are Americans so stupid that they don't recognize this guy's a bum?

Resonance in Leaders

That's a fact. Because if you think about what the role of leaders in society have been, for example in the United States, or in some cases of some Europeans, you find that the leading figure,—as speaking to the population around,—that these figures have a certain resonance, which attracts the audience very much as like what just happened here. The idea of "tuning in" on coherence.

So the easiest thing to do, is if somebody is really twisting everything around, and you don't like it,—not because you have some prejudice, but because it doesn't fit your idea of what a human being should say, in order to propose a policy question to an audience,—and therefore I think the best experience is exactly that. That when people are able to convey concepts which resonate within the mind of an audience, you have to pay attention to that. And when it doesn't resonate, you have to say, "uh-oh, we've got a problem."

Maybe it's something that can be corrected, but the likelihood is that there's something wrong with the works, if you can't get that kind of resonance.

Q: Hello. I'm from Turkey, and I'm a student. I am learning English. If you can't understand me, you can tell me. It's okay? My name is S—.

I have a question, one question. We have so many problems. One of them is ISIS. Second one, economic problems: What are the economic problems in Turkey? So many factors turn up, so many factors to try to correct now. And also young people cannot find jobs in Turkey. Other problems: our government killed 200 Kurdish people in the last four months, and also some fascist Turkish people are killing Kurdish people, too. And governments have suffered [allowed] them. Also, Kurdish people killed so many soldiers, and these soldiers' ages are like 21, 22 years old.

What is the question? I need peace in Turkey. Also in the Middle East. Some countries tried communism in Europe. It didn't work. And also, capitalism, it doesn't work for us. I need new systems, new economic systems for my country, meaning Arab countries also.

The question: What new economic system is available for me? Also, what is the way? Got it?

> So, we are now at a point of a very evil condition of mankind. However, there are certain movements which are coming into shape, which can bring about a kind of harmony among different parts of human culture, and that I think is what the objective has to be. Because each part of society does have its own characteristics. But the characteristics we're looking for are those which are harmonious, harmonious for that population.

Harmony in Culture

LaRouche: Okay, you've got quite a list of things implicitly, as your concern in this matter. I understand what the variegation is in the expression, because it's valid.

The point is, we're living in a dissonant world. That's the first thing. The United States is dissonant. It's a terrible place, not because it's the United States, but because we have Obama in it. And we had some Bushes in it, and they weren't burning—maybe they should have been burning—but the Bush family is not very good. It never was.

And we've had many bad Presidents as well, back in our history.

The problem is this: We're trying to get some kind of harmony within society. Now, obviously, I know the Turkish situation. I'm not an expert in experience in Turkey, but I know what the problem is. We see the ISIS problem cuts into there. We see the whole thing. We see what happened in Africa, northern Africa—same thing.

So, we are now at a point of a very evil condition of mankind. However, there are certain movements which are coming into shape, which can bring about a kind of harmony among different parts of human culture, and that I think is what the objective has to be. Because each part of society does have its own characteristics. But the characteristics we're looking for are those which are harmonious, harmonious for that population.

And it's a moral question. It's a question of satisfaction. It's not just that you want to have your own language and speak it. You want the *ideas* that that language conveys to be harmonious with other parts of humanity.

Now we're not doing too well right now on that, on

this basis. But we can focus on the intention that we shall come to that kind of harmonious relationship among different qualities of human population. And that's our best shot. It's the idea of going for the harmonious expression, among different languages, different particular cultures, different experiences. But we can bring about the harmonious inter-relationship within and among those nations, and their cultures.

Q: [follow-up] It sounds very good, but the problem is our government, also our system. How can I do that? I am a student. I have some contacts. I have some friends. I am socialist, actually, and we have a party actually. And what can I do?

Everything has Changed

LaRouche: Now you've got this case already there, and Putin, President Putin, has moved from where people thought he was going to stay, and he moved in to try to clean up the ISIS problem and so forth, in order to bring about harmony. Because we know that there is a disharmony in that part of the world, but we also know that with some corrections, we can bring about a relatively harmonious relationship.

We're seeing aspects of that right now. We see it in Europe.

For example: Look. Here you have this terrible threat of general warfare throughout the nations of the North Atlantic area, both sides. And suddenly, something wonderful happened. Germany stepped forward under the pressure essentially of Putin, President Putin, stepped forward and began to move other parts of Europe, and other parts of the world, into an attempt at harmony. We've seen too much disharmony in Europe—there are some places in Europe that are not harmonious by any means, right now.

But the tendency, the attempt to form a harmonious relationship among different cultures, which have different characteristics,—that is in process. And I think the question is: Are we going to be able to carry out what we know we have as a potential? Do we have the ability to bring about that kind of potential when the nations come together?

I think the ultimate result is the fact that mankind is going to have to change. Mankind *will* change. We see it in South America. We see it in India. We see it in other nations there. And I think we're on the verge of such a change. Putin has played a very key role in this, because he upset everything. And by upsetting it, he created an opportunity to bring about harmony—it doesn't exist yet—but we see it coming. We saw that Putin moved into a direction that people thought he was *not* going move into. And by moving into that, in that sector there, what he did has now broken out and created an impetus for grave reforms in that whole region of nations.

Prospects for General Peace

Now I think the options are good. They're not guaranteed, but we have enough good options, to know that it is possible to pull something off like this now. It may take a little time, but we know we're on a different package. We see it in Germany. We saw it first in Germany breaking out. We've seen it now in France. We've seen it in other locations.

kremlin.ru

Seeking harmony among cultures: President Vladimir Putin, in the center on the left side of the table, conducts a dialogue with Russia's Muslim spiritual administrations in October 2013.

For example: Look. Here you have this terrible threat of general warfare throughout the nations of the North Atlantic area, both sides. And suddenly, something wonderful happened. Germany stepped forward under the pressure essentially of Putin, President Putin, and stepped forward and began to move other parts of Europe, and other parts of the world, into an attempt at harmony. We've seen too much disharmony in Europe— there are some places in Europe that are not harmonious by any means, right now.

So it means there's a *change in the winds* of progress. And so, I think all nations will have an opportunity.

For example, we have the Kra Canal progress,—just take that as an example of a reference, now, right now, I was involved in pushing what was called the Kra Canal. And this reform which we worked on, was not carried out. Japan was working to support this thing, and it could have worked. It would move the transport of goods in the southern region of the world, and bring that about in such a way that we could actually make a *great* improvement in terms of maritime traffic and in relations among nations. We have things like that underway now as possibilities, and in some degree, partly acceptable. But it's there: The options now for man, are options which go beyond anything that mankind has had for a very long time. It's still a tough time; it's still dangerous, but there is the sign of something which is good. We just have to work with it and hope we can win.

Q: [follow-up] All right, we'll see everything, everything will change in Europe and Asia and everywhere; it doesn't matter. But every day people are dying. It's government's problem. I have to focus first of all on my country. After that I can focus on global problems. Of course, I have to think about global problems because we are living on the world, and...

We Can Do It

LaRouche: Look, the best thing is—you've got to bring people into,—or some people at least,— you've got to bring them into harmony. And therefore, while they may retain different particular characteristics in their behavior, the point is that there must be a harmonious relationship. And that's what we're seeing right now with Russia's intrusion, in trying to save part of this whole area, which includes Turkey. We have to do that. It's an obligation. It's a moral one. And my view is, we have the potential in the fairly short term, of *possibly* bringing about a general peace throughout the planet. That is now possible. It doesn't mean it's guaranteed, but it means the winds are blowing in that direction. The question is whether we can keep the windstorm going up.

Q: [follow-up] Yeah. We have to, actually, we must do that. I know that. But...

We have to: we must do it. OK, but I'm not government, I'm not God, I'm not anyone, I'm just a student; I have just some ideas, that's all. But if I don't do any-

NASA

Harmony in action: Astronauts currently on the International Space Station. This picture was released this September in connection with the visit of the first Dane in space, Andreas Mogensen, seen bottom right.

thing, who's going to do something? I have to do something as a student. What can I do?

LaRouche: We can do it! We are trying to do this on a global basis. We are trying to change the whole situation of the planet right now, the human occupation of the planet. In China, in India, in many other nations there is a very important development. What we all

---

We can do it! We are trying to do this on a global basis. We are trying to change the whole situation of the planet right now, the human occupation of the planet. In China, in India, in many other nations there is a very important development. What we all have to do is bring a certain *harmony* among those nations which are trying to converge on harmony as such, on a general harmony.

---

have to do is bring a certain *harmony* among those nations which are trying to converge on harmony as such, on a general harmony.

And you're a student? All right, you know exactly what you want. You know the kind of life you want to have *in your head*, and your neighbor's. And you can achieve that. It's been done before in society; it can be done right now.

Q: [follow-up] All right. I'll try. Thank you. [applause]

Q: I have been involved most of my life with music, although I'm not a musician. That's harmony I'm talking about. So when we have harmony, from the beginning, then we should have harmony going forward. I know the technology of today is wonderful. But why have we removed harmony from our lives by removing beautiful music, the Classics, all the instruments that were quite beautiful: the violins, the violas, the cellos, all of these things,—and we go to beating drums? Which I always thought was for making war. [LaRouche laughs] I don't know if I'm right or wrong. At my age, I'm beginning to think maybe I learned the wrong thing growing up. I'm 80 plus. I won't tell you what the plus is, but it's plus.

So, explain to me where we've gone wrong, because I remember the Classics—Shakespeare. I remember the music Classics, including the later ones of Brahms. So where are we now, where we beat drums for war? Explain it; I don't know.

Only One Real Scientist

LaRouche: Well, I think you should be more optimistic. Or at least I think there are grounds for you to be more optimistic on this subject.

First, you have two problems. We had a progressive movement on the part of the United States, in parts of the experience of the United States, during the 1800s. At the end of that period, what we had was the introduction of a fairly evil influence in terms of the government of the United States. And Bertrand Russell jumped in on that, and Bertrand Russell created evil, *pure evil*, throughout his entire life. And what happened is, we used to have science, but Bertrand Russell came along and virtually destroyed science.

And there was one man in the whole kit and caboodle who was really loyal to the principle of science—Einstein. He was the only person in the whole century, who manifested a really true appreciation of what the meaning of his objectives were. And he died, but in the meantime we have gone through a destruction of the moral and intellectual development of the citizens of the United States, both in the Twentieth Century and in the Twenty-First Century now. We are destroying our children, our young people; we are destroying our aging people. We are reducing them to bitterness and fear.

So that we've come to a time when a great change has to occur. And I believe that what we're trying to do now, with the new agreement which is coming in the next week, this coming week,—this turn can be the opening which forces the opening of a new view of the planet.

You see what happened in Germany. Recently Germany seemed to be almost hopeless—the Germans and what they were going to do. Suddenly, the leaders of Germany,—that is, the senior leaders of Germany,—suddenly organized something which became infectious. It spread to other parts of Europe. All these people were being thrown into the water to be drowned or to be killed otherwise, and the leaders of Germany *moved*, together with Putin, to try to remove this problem and correct this error.

We don't know how much we can count on a certain success, but we know that success is possible now. And everything that's beautiful for people who know that

The West-Eastern Divan orchestra, established in 1999 by Argentine-Israeli conductor Daniel Barenboim and the late Palestinian-American academic Edward Said, to promote harmony in the war-torn Middle East region. Here, Barenboim with the orchestra in Salzburg, Austria in May 2013.

the one thing on that which I think has to be put on the record for this purpose. It's the fact that we are in a situation right now, with this United Nations operation in place: I think we have entered into a period of opportunity, and a certain zeal involved in that. I think that in the coming week, and the week after that, and maybe the week after that, we're going to find there's a fundamental sweeping change in terms of many things about the United States, and also certain other parts of the world. [Applause.]

was beautiful, and always wanted that beautiful kind of thing to come knocking on the door, I think we are approaching a possibility with that question. I don't think—you know, I'm 93 years of age, [laughs] so maybe I'm senior to you, and therefore, I think maybe I can say something about that.

A Period of Opportunity

Q: [follow-up] When you mentioned Einstein, I did remember he played the violin quite well.

LaRouche: [laughs heartily] Yes, of course! He did more than that.

Q: [follow-up] ...we go forward, rather than backwards. Thank you.

Q: Hello, I'm C—from Brooklyn. I have a comment, and then maybe an idea. September 17th was the Constitution's birthday. The Constitution is 231 years old. I know that we have to fight hard to reinstate Glass-Steagall. But I think while we are holding the sign that says, "Reinstate Glass-Steagall" we need to hold another sign that says "Reinstate the Constitution." That's it. [Applause.]

LaRouche: [laughs] Okay. Well, I can answer on

Q: I'm R—from Staten Island. And I'm a student of history, I work in a National Park, and recently President Obama changed the name of Mt. McKinley, and also there's discussion and suggestion that Alexander Hamilton be taken off the ten-dollar bill. What's

> We are in a situation right now, with this United Nations operation in place: I think we have entered into a period of opportunity, and a certain zeal involved in that. I think that in the coming week, and the week after that, and maybe the week after that, we're going to find there's a fundamental sweeping change in terms of many things about the United States, and also certain other parts of the world.

implied by these actions, and what do you think of them?

Alexander Hamilton

LaRouche: Well, very simply, Alexander Hamilton was the founder of the United States. His role, of course, was manifold, but his key role was in the Philadelphia convention, which preceded the formation of the actual Constitution of the United States. He'd played a key role in shaping the principles, or actually the four key

The conclusion of the Peace of Westphalia in 1648 marked the end of the orgy of blood called the Thirty Years War, and established the principle of nation states collaborating for the "benefit of the other." This painting by Dutch artist Gerard ter Borch shows the ratification of the Treaty of Münster which finalized the agreement.

economic principles of the United States; he was the one who induced the President of the United States to become the President, the first President of United States, Washington.

Then he was shot! And then things weren't so good. And the people in the United States at that time who were evil, who were promoters of slavery, and a whole bunch of them were promoters of slavery,—about four of them in the Presidency at one swoop. And then we got a great President back in there. And then next we had a real bum, evil bum, who liked to kill Indians, things like that. And we have a very poor record, with few exceptions by our Presidents in that era, until Abraham Lincoln became President. Now that was good. But then they killed him. And by killing him, they disrupted the entire effort of Abraham Lincoln.

Then later on there were a lot of ups and downs and so forth. We had a great general who led the fight, the warfare to defeat the enemy, to defeat the British, in fact. And then we had a great President here and there. But they get scarcer and scarcer.

Abraham Lincoln would have been happy to see some of these things. And certainly our greatest President, Franklin Roosevelt, achieved great things. And we had a few Presidents who were not too bad. But then, recently, we've had nothing but terrible Presidents. We could enjoy some relief from that sort of thing. But that's the sort of history of the United States in short. And Alexander Hamilton is essentially the monitor of that history of our nation, of our republic.

Bernie Sanders

Q: Good afternoon, Mr. La-Rouche. This is R—from Brooklyn. On Friday we did a deployment at 43rd Street and Sixth Avenue, and at any given time we had five to seven people there, and at the same time, Sen. Bernie Sanders had a Town Hall Meeting at the same location, and I was giving out Glass-Steagall leaflets, and there was less resistance than in the past. It seems like a lot of people are hearing more about Glass-Steagall. Several people made a comment to me, "I'm on your side, I think they should bring back Glass-Steagall." And I heard from some of Bernie Sanders' supporters, that at his meeting he supported and recommended Glass-Steagall. How do you see Bernie Sanders at this time?

LaRouche: well, I see him in a positive light. How far he's going to get with his election campaign I don't know. This is the very tricky period. We have a couple of people who are Presidential candidates who would be useful. I realize we need a new Presidential system, and we need certain protections to ensure that those things will be handled properly, so we won't get the usual kind of swindle we've had recently. Because this system now, of recent Presidents and recent procedures, are not decent operations.

And what he's trying to do,—I sympathize with what he's trying to do in this thing. I don't know how successful he could be, but I see what he's doing. This question has to be really dealt with.

We must absolutely get rid of Obama, and anything like him, from the United States. We have people in the Congress who don't belong there; people in the Senate who don't belong there. Because, they, in a sense are

We must absolutely get rid of Obama, and anything like him, from the United States.... We need a new Presidential system, which means with a President and a coherent team around that President. We need that now. We don't want these jokers we're getting from other locations. We don't.

crooks, or are feeble,—feeble in their moral qualifications.

We need a new Presidential system, which means a President and a coherent team around that President. We need that now. We don't want these jokers we're getting from other locations. We don't. And what he's doing is a contribution to expressing what must be considered. And I think he's generally on the right track. As I say, I don't know how much qualification he has to actually achieve the actual nomination and election. But I think his efforts have merit, and should be treated accordingly.

Wall Street Hopelessly Bankrupt

Q: Good afternoon, Mr. LaRouche. This is J—from Brooklyn, New York. I'm approaching things a little differently today. I was recently speaking with some friends of mine, and we were talking about the things that we need to do *when* Glass-Steagall is put in place—not *if* it is put in place, but *when* it is achieved.

And some words came up that seemed to evoke a lot of emotion in people. And one of those things that I thought was a good idea to do, when Glass-Steagall is put in place, is to have a Manhattan Project, like the Manhattan Project of old that produced a nuclear bomb, the A-bomb, but in this case we would produce nuclear energy. We're going to need nuclear energy to power all those buildings that are going to be vacant, that you talked about once before, that we'll need to put hospitals into, and schools, and other residential buildings and homes for people. And kick Trump out and put

people in homes that they can afford, and we could use those buildings for that.

Well, we were talking about this new Manhattan Project that would not be a destructive A-bomb, but would be to get nuclear energy on the table, to actually come together with scientists to produce this new amount of energy that we're going to need to power New York City. People are afraid of this "nuclear" word, nuclear energy. And I just thought about it for a minute, and I'd like you to kind of put in perspective why there is such a fear of the idea of nuclear energy. I know that with the Cold War and all that business, we were brainwashed into thinking that "nuclear" means something really terrible. But we know we have the technology to produce nuclear power plants, and to produce them safely. And so if you could kind of tell us a little bit about what you know on this nuclear thing?

LaRouche: Well, I can do also the other part of what you made in your remarks, and take the two of them together. First of all, Wall Street is presently hopelessly bankrupt. That is, there is no way that Wall Street can continue to live. It can't. Just look at the figures, and

White House/Chuck Kennedy

Dissonance in the White House: Obama presides over a "Memphis Soul" performance in the East Room in April 2013.

go over this period where they have this "easing" story; I don't know if you were following this "easing" story: Every week we were getting a new "easing" story. And what was this? It was nothing but a fraud, a complete fraud.

Now, Wall Street is actually hopelessly bankrupt.

Now, Wall Street is actually hopelessly bankrupt. There is no way in which Wall Street can actually exist. There would have to be a Nazi occupation for Wall Street to survive, and it might not even survive then.

There is no way in which Wall Street can actually exist. There would have to be a Nazi occupation for Wall Street to survive, and it might not even survive then.

So that's the first thing. So therefore, it's going to go! Now, we're trying to get Wall Street shut down, permanently and in a peaceful way, because we don't want a big fight. We want it to just be absolutely bankrupted, thrown out of office, thrown out of their positions, because all they're committing is frauds. There is no justification for the defense of Wall Street. It's a disease; it's an enemy of mankind.

How to Rebuild

So now, at the same time, what are we faced with? What is our construction method? How're we going reconstruct what has been destroyed by Wall Street, and by Wall Street's accomplices? All right, well, that's simple, and you're right: it is nuclear power. Right now, we have some very bad news, not relevant to this directly, but indirectly. First of all, we have people who are trying to produce a reduction of the population, and it's being done by a Pope; and the Pope is out to reduce the population by a method of mass murder, and that's what it is, there's no doubt of it. The governor of California is now a spokesman for this kind of mass murder.

Now therefore, what we have to do then, is we have to say: "Look, we have to increase the power per capita of human beings, the power of creativity, to enable mankind both to sustain larger populations, to correct evils, and so forth." Our education system stinks, and has for a long period of time. You know, you have some people who are teaching properly, but the institutions don't do that; they don't practice that.

We are a degenerate nation, and I think at the time that President Ronald Reagan was shot, but lived afterward, the effect of his being shot ruined what became his re-election. Therefore at that time of the shooting of Ronald Reagan, who I was actually working for,—he was a good guy, but he really was weakened by the shooting of him, and so the Bush family took over. We've had the Bushes; the Bushes are kind of stupid, except for the grandfather. They were just stupid; he was evil. The effect was about the same, I guess.

But anyway, the point is the development of higher forms of energy. We are now in a process where we're going into the new space operations; we're going into a new layer of future science, and also nearby space within the Galaxy. So we are now working on developing a Galactic System which will be controlled, directly or indirectly, by mankind as a developing system. That is now a feasible proposition. It is not something we are able, yet, to work, but we do know the water system of the United States and Earth in general, depends upon this water system of the Galactic System. So in order to do that, you have to go into the nuclear areas; otherwise you can't accomplish that project.

So these are things which you're talking about, which are highly important, as well as feasible. It's going to take a little work to get it moving, but that's possible.

The Fraud of Wall Street

Q: Hi, Mr. LaRouche, this is R—from Bergen County, New Jersey. I preemptively apologize if this question is not well formulated because I just started thinking about it.

LaRouche: [laughs] OK!

Q: [follow-up] There was an article on the website where the first part of the article says that in a Glass-Steagall system of physical economy, prices will have to be completely reconsidered, and adjusted, if I read that correctly. In other words, pricing in a non-Glass-Steagall system seems to be based on what the market will bear, which means that prices are manipulated, unnecessary goods, entertainment, for example, is created and purchased through brainwashing operations; quantitative easing creates bubbles, and monopolies and cartels are formed, etc., in order to set prices at whatever

Harmony among nations: The construction of the floor of the Tokamak pit at the International Experimental Thermonuclear Reaction (ITER) site in southern France. The work is being conducted by scientists and engineers from the European Union, China, Russia, Japan, India, South Korea, and the United States.

iter.org

levels people can use to collect the most possible money, because money is a primary value in a non-Glass-Steagall system.

One can argue, I would argue, that a lot of pricing that's being done in a non-Glass-Steagall system is artificial and false because they're not based on productive value; they're based on speculation. So if money is the only value, and it doesn't matter if you're selling steel or if you're selling pornography, whatever is going to be the most profitable is what you're going to go after.

Do you have anything to say on the readjustment of pricing in what hopefully will become the Glass-Steagall physical economy system?

LaRouche: Sure! I do. The facts of the matter are sufficient; it's not a matter of speculation, it's a matter of facts, and the need to recognize those facts. All right, so Wall Street is hopelessly bankrupt right now. There is no basis for the sustaining of the existence of the Wall Street system at this time. If you look at the so-called easing program that was going along for some years,

every week, a new "easing," a new "easing" program, well, what was this? This was pure inflation. The easing program was pure inflation and fraudulent.

Then we got into a later period, where that whole thing has no capability of surviving; no intrinsic ability to survive. So the thing is, if we act, and we act on the basis of a government finding that Wall Street is a fraud, complete fraud, today, and if the United States acts on that basis, *there is no more Wall Street*. Wall Street disappears.

New International Negotiations

Now, that would by my joy, to watch this process, but I think it should occur anyway, whether I'm there to see it or not. But we have to get the United States free of this kind of great fraud. It's a complete British-style fraud that's being played on us! We are being destroyed as a nation, by the effects of what is done by Wall Street. And Wall Street has no merit, it has no reason to *exist*; there's no justification for it to exist. And people who sponsor this in the Congress, should be shut down in the Congress! Because we can't have that any more.

And as our speaker earlier said, the introduction of the proper higher order of energies, nuclear energies, and super-nuclear energies,—these things are absolutely essential; and we have to fight against the fact that there's a scheme to try to reduce the members of the population of the United States right now, in particular, to kill us by these methods. The governor of California is an advocate of mass murder against the citizens of not only the United States, but also of California as such. He's very active on this thing.

So these problems have to be treated accordingly. There are evils, such as these and others, like the drug problems, like the lack of a competent school system

> **But I think we're at a point,—what is the point? The point is, now we have a new international agreement in the making. This agreement, this negotiation can be the mechanism by which we change things very quickly during this period of international negotiations. By doing that we can change almost everything that has to be changed. All we have to do is get the people to see,—and I think many people do see,—many governments see, many parts of the world governments, they see this has been a terrible problem, and they're approaching a point where they're about ready to do something about that.**

any more. The education system is poisonous; the culture, the cultural factors in most parts of the United States, are terrible. We're going to have to rebuild!

But I think we're at a point,—what is the point? The point is, now we have a new international agreement in the making. This agreement, this negotiation can be the mechanism by which we change things very quickly during this period of international negotiations. By doing that we can change almost everything that has to be changed. All we have to do is get the people to see,—and I think many people do see,—many governments see, many parts of the world governments, they see this has been a terrible problem, and they're approaching a point where they're about ready to do something about that.

So I think our function here, in our more modest work, in Massachusetts, or other similar places,—that the time has come that we can actually do something about this. The option is there and the means is understood. I'm familiar with the means that can be used. I think we can do it. And I think this period, or this period of this international event for the next coming weeks,—this does present the option of getting a sweeping change in these conditions.

A Fundamental Change

Q: Hello, Mr. LaRouche, H—from the Bronx. I appreciate this discussion on the economy; we in the Bronx, we have a lot of problems with housing and it seems under the existing conditions, almost impossible to build new housing. We have other problems with the Greenies, but I'm trying to get to the point of your presentation, which is the international agreement. Do you think that Mr. Putin of Russia and forces

that he has at his control can defeat ISIS, the Islamic State, in Syria and other places?

We have to be concerned about the strange superpowers of the so-called ISIS thing, and why it continues to expand. We are told that there there's a coalition out there that's fighting ISIS; we had the Kurds that won their little battle in Kobane; but then there were certain setbacks, which may be to do with some of the things going on in Turkey at this time.

But anyway, what's up? Because it seems to be good, but then not so good.

LaRouche: No, it's good right now. What happened is, President Putin changed his program in a couple of phases, including being a sponsor of a march [Victory Day parade September 3] in China; and this was a real military power show by China. But Putin was one of the people who set it up! But immediately

tjgtheatre.org

Charles Dutoit and the Philadelphia Orchestra at a concert in Tianjin, China in June 2012.

after that, Putin also moved to deal with the other part of the show.

So now, inside the present system, Putin has moved things south! And is going to take over. And what's happened in Germany, is that the leaders of Germany have also supported this in their own way. Officials in France, have adopted that; others have adopted that policy.

Right now, there has been a fundamental change in the alignment of major forces, in terms of the trans-Atlantic region in particular, but also beyond. So now that which you want to happen, it probably can happen. Now we're having this great celebration among the nations, where they're coming now to their seasonal bit on that subject, and it's probable that they will succeed. And therefore, these things are achievements which are being done in part by Putin, who's been a leader in this operation.

Great Projects Beckon

And you see this whole change. You just watch what I've seen in the past three or four weeks, the *change* in terms of the trans-Atlantic community. It's big. I think that this new event coming in the following weeks to come right now,—I think that's the occasion for bringing that issue more to the fore, and bringing it around to certain actuality; I think we can do it.

Q: Hi Lyn: Bill Roberts [of the LaRouche PAC Policy Committee] from Detroit,—from the Galaxy, but Detroit, specifically.

So, on Tuesday, there will be an *EIR* seminar and press conference to announce the release of the special report that's been published by *Executive Intelligence Review*, "'Global Warming' Scare Is Population Reduction, not Science"; and this will be part of a series of interventions going into the UN General Assembly meeting.

You raised, I think importantly, the connection within the Twentieth Century of really the twin evils of Wall Street and the Green population reduction/climate change fraud. It's often the case in popular political terms that oftentimes people will be soft on one of those, and see the other one as evil. Europeans are more infested by the Greenie ideology; I wonder if you could just address the importance of what can actually be done along the lines of the defeat of the British Monar-

The Schiller Institute Manhattan chorus, in rehearsal on Sept. 17, with conductor Diane Sare.

Members of the Manhattan Project study Kepler's harmonies prior to the discussion with Lyndon LaRouche, on Sept. 19, 2015.

EIRNS/Margaret Greenspan

EIRNS/Diane Sare

chy which occurred at Copenhagen [UN COP15] in 2009, and the importance of this particular question in terms of what has to be done to actually bring together a harmonic association of principle in the upcoming United Nations General Assembly.

LaRouche: I think you just put your finger on the issue: The General Assembly. That assembly, I think, is pregnant with intention to make some radical changes, or what would seem radical changes. Look at the crisis of France, for example, and you have the crisis of Germany; other crises in Europe. The crises which you see in other areas, in the intermediate areas; the operations and opportunities we see in areas such as the Kra Canal project. The Kra Canal project, which is a very feasible thing and has been; I would push for this thing, and actually some Japanese institutions wanted to get the channel through the Kra Canal; and the Kra Canal channel would change the character of much of the international trade in the Pacific and related regions, and the Oceania area.

The Mind Is the Future

So all these things are *there*; they're now ready to go! And we simply have to find the catalyst, and the catalyst I think involves the General Assembly. I think the General Assembly defines the option of launching

exactly what most people would think is impossible, but what I see is very possible. I can't say it's guaranteed, but I can say it's very, very possible. And if you could give us a few weeks before we close down the General Assembly, I think within that period you're going to find some very important action, gratifying action, on this matter.

Q: [follow-up] Great, thank you.

Q: [Megan Beets of the LaRouche PAC Science Team] Hi, Lyn. You saw the opening of our [music] session today, when we were doing some work on Kepler and the issue of harmony and the origination of harmony in the human mind. So I was just wondering if you could maybe say a few more things about that, but I wanted to put it in the context of what you had brought up in a discussion that we had had earlier this week on Tuesday, where you were insistent that man's not a creature of the senses; he doesn't live from the present into the future, but the creative impulses of the human mind are in the future. They make and create the future. So I was wondering if you could say a few things about that in the context of what we were discussing today?

LaRouche: Yes, I understand exactly. No, the issue here is: what is the nature of mankind, and how does mankind's nature differ from that of animals? That's the issue. And it's a very important one. Because only mankind is capable of being mankind; others are just animals. Now that doesn't mean the animals are bad creatures, but it means they're not human. They don't have the essential qualities of humanity. And so, this defines the concern on that account.

Human Immortality

I'll keep it short: The point is, do you believe that there's a meaning to the death of a human being? Do you think that there's a positive meaning in the death of what had been a living human being? Because there's no animal that can meet that standard; no animal, no species of animal. Only the human species has a reason for existing in the future.

In other words, you live a life which comes to a point of death, and is there a future of that person? Or is there some continuity of the presence of that person? In a good human society, a real human society, there is an immortal principle: that the dead, when they've lived an appropriate life, will bring about the discovery of creativity, the discovery of creativities, which give mankind a higher standard of achievement than mankind has ever achieved before, in that circle.

And therefore, you have a quality of immortality of the dead human beings, which can be achieved, because they live a life, and when they died, they are able to have supplied a contribution to the future of mankind,—and only human beings can do that. And the shame is, when human beings don't do that, when the human beings think they can't do that. And the point is, they should all be developed to be able to make that kind of contribution to the future.

Mankind is essentially, virtually, the immortal species. And even death of the individual does not end the meaning of their life, if they give a meaning to their life.

If they're creative, if they make discoveries that mankind has not known before, they make steps in progress in that direction. All of these things are that virtue which is specific to the human being's opportunities. Mankind is the only immortal species of which we know.

Speed: Lyn, I believe we're at the end of the questions, and I—not so much by way of conclusion, but I want to bring up something: A friend of yours, whom you invoked at your birthday. Some of us from New Jersey gave you a recording of the work of Bill Warfield. And some people wouldn't have a reason to know, but William Warfield was one of the members of the board of the Schiller Institute, and got to know Lyn, actually. One of the very first things we did, which I think was in May of 1994, that's when Lyn met Bill Warfield.

Now, many people don't know who he is, but he was one of the great singers of the Twentieth Century, and he wrote an autobiography called *My Music and My Life*, and on this question of dissonance and harmony, I wanted to bring something up and have Lyn respond to it; because Warfield compares how he dealt with the racism of not being allowed to sing on the stage of the Metropolitan Opera, and how others of his contemporaries didn't deal with racism. And he makes an important point, which I think is something, Lyn, you may want to comment on.

So Bill says this—Bill was born in 1920; he was a World War II veteran. He says: "When we remember the Civil Rights revolution of the 1950s, we forget that it got its momentum in the 1940s." He then talks about a friend of his named William Marshall who was also an actor. He says, "Marshall was up to date on all these movements, and his involvement was an important part of my education. In particular, he was following the ups and downs of Paul Robeson's career. I was particularly interested to know more about that. Where Marshall and I were of different mentalities, was in our perceptions of personal slights due to racism: I was generally oblivious; he was easily insulted. In Boston, in Cleveland, in Chicago, it could be as simple as buying a newspaper from the corner stand. He would look at me with a kind of wonder. 'You're very naïve,' he'd say, 'Look around you. Did you see the way that person looked at you?' and he would laugh a bitter laugh."

Bill says, "Marshall was often right. I had simply not noticed before he mentioned it, and would probably never have paid any attention. I would ignore it; he would fume. That was the climate that was always around us then. Neither William Marshall nor I were on the barricades of the movement. Each of us in our own way worked out our commitment on a different kind of stage. But temperamentally, you could say that Bill Marshall and Bill Warfield represented opposite extremes within our own band of the spectrum. He didn't miss a single nuance of even unconscious racism; I

Mankind is essentially, virtually, the immortal species. And even death of the individual does not end the meaning of their life, if they give a meaning to their life; if they're creative, if they make discoveries that mankind has not known before; they make steps in progress in that direction. All of these things are that virtue which is specific to the human being's opportunities. Mankind is the only immortal species of which we know.

---

shrugged it off. Racism was going to be the racist's handicap, not mine."

Now, I put this here, Lyn, because you've referenced harmony, dissonance; Obama as a dissonant personality, and so on. And Bill—I was listening to a recording he did of the *Four Serious Songs*, Brahms, that whole first one particularly. And as we go out, as we conclude, I just wanted to see if you might want to say something about, not so much him, but this issue of what it takes to be creative in the face of great adversity, and how, when we go into this UN session, we might be able to overcome any of those problems any of us have?

LaRouche: You have to really study Bill Warfield's behavior. Look, he was very, very clear in his sense of what his mission was. He did not feel that he was somehow shortcoming in any of the things he did. He was not a bitter man as such. He was a man who could become angry, but if you know what his personal life was like, and what he went through in the process of this life he lived, you see a man who was not reacting personally. He was reacting impersonally, on the question of music, on the question of art, on the question of everything,—yes, race, too.

But it wasn't like an angry thing; not a rage thing. It was something that was *plain fact*. Everything he did was *plain fact*. Even the abuse he was subjected to under certain condition: plain fact! Because he devoted himself to his mission, and that's what made the difference.

He was a person who lived and died for his mission, which was largely music. He performed in Europe, he performed in the United States. He was a major figure in the trans-Atlantic community, in his musical abilities. But he did not have the fault which many ambitious singers and others would have under the same circumstances.

He was a friend to me, in my relationship to him; we were partners in spirit. We worked together, we talked together, and he was a friend. [applause]

Speed: Thank you, Lyn. So if you'd like to give us any summary; I think we got a very clear idea that you think we have a mission for this week, but if there's anything you'd like to say in closing, we'd be happy to hear it.

LaRouche: Well, fine. Look, this is the great assembly that's going to be brought out over the weekend, and this is probably one of the most important, precious opportunities, to get mankind out of the mess that mankind has been in up to this point.

Much of the world does not want to continue the kind of things that mankind has been subjected to recently and for a long time. And I think, that if we succeed,—and I think we *can* succeed,—with the General Assembly, because with what we've seen in Europe in terms of changes in temperament in Europe, in parts of Europe, what we've seen in other parts of the planet, it is now possible to make radical changes in devotion to service, which had not been experienced by me, very much for a very long time. And now it's just happened, recently. It came to the surface at the time that President Putin made a shift in his policy, and upset everything that Obama was working for.

And I think that the dumping of Obama under this process, is the thing that is required, if you want to save humanity from a horrible fate. I think a lot of the world would agree with that. They may not think of Obama himself as the focal point of their concern; but whenever they would see something smells like Obama politically, they would have the same reaction: Get this guy out of here. [applause]

Speed: Thank you, Lyn. And that is the conclusion, for today.

Renewed Prospects for Kra Canal— Project for Benefit of Whole World

Sept. 19—The last segment of the LaRouche PAC Sept. 18 webcast was devoted to the renewed prospect of developing a canal across the Isthmus of Kra in Thailand. See the full video here.

Jason Ross: For a final topic today, we're going to talk about the discussions that have been taking place among Russia, South Korea, and China shaping up towards the creation of a North Asia Development Bank that would include the Koreas, Russia, China, and Japan. This comes in the context of the Eastern Economic Forum in Vladivostok, held directly after the Victory Day celebrations in China at the beginning of this month, where Russian President Putin and Korean President Park were very prominent guests of President Xi.

Lyndon LaRouche responded to the development around the possibility of this North Asian Development Bank by stressing the necessity for building the Kra Canal, a project whose recent planning goes back to the 1980s, to build a canal across the Isthmus of Kra in Thailand, relieving the overburdened Straits of Malacca, providing new transportation routes and development for the region, especially today, as seen in the context of the New Silk Road.

I'd like to ask Benjamin Deniston, who has some remarks on this topic, to tell us about the Kra Canal.

Instead of Wall Street's Idea of Money

Ben Deniston: Thanks, Jason. Just to open up, I think this is an excellent counterpoint to what we just discussed with the insanity of Wall Street, and the Wall Street system: the Wall Street idea of money, this money system that is now blowing out, where there's this religious belief in the value of money *per se*, and this insanity around trying to defend this bubble, which is full of financial assets which don't have any value.

Now you contrast that with what China is doing in collaboration with Russia, the BRICS nations, their other allies, other nations they're working with around the world, in this completely new orientation, where they're creating institutions, new financial institutions: like the Asia Infrastructure Investment Bank; or the discussion of a prospective North Asian Development Bank.

So, new financial institutions, new financial structures, to deal with what some people might call money, but which I think Mr. LaRouche would define, more rigorously, as credit, as distinct from simply a monetary policy. Institutions to provide credit, specifically for projects like the Kra Canal.

Now, if we can get the first graphic up on the screen: **(Figure 1)**. We're particularly talking about a region in

FIGURE 1

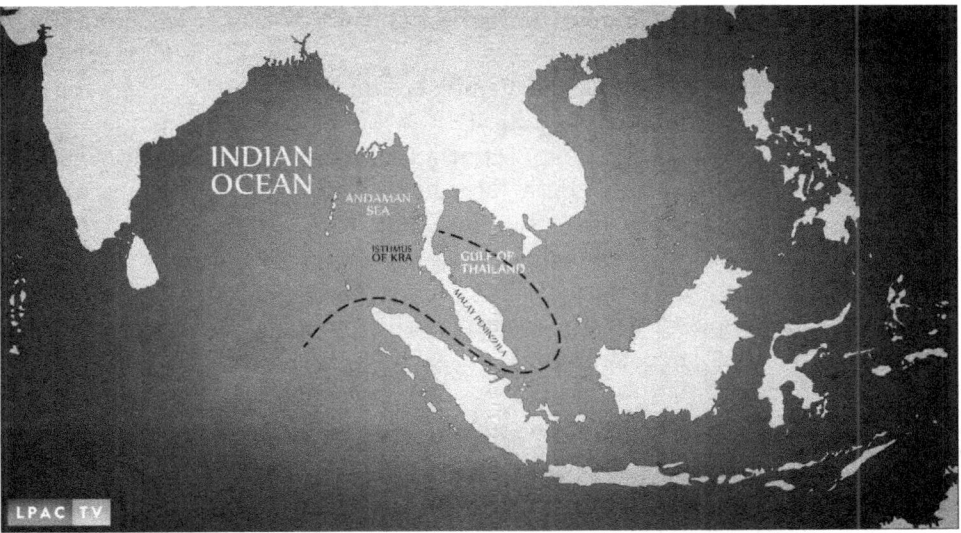

Southeast Asia. Currently all shipping that goes from East Asia—from China, from South Korea, from Japan, from this entire region, which has a substantial amount of economic activity—any of the shipping from this region that goes to India, to the Mediterranean, up into Europe, goes through [the Straits of Malacca]—and the discussion on China's work on the New Maritime Silk Road, which is the maritime aspect of their Silk Road project, covers this exact same territory as well.

The shipping goes through a very congested bottleneck, which you can see displayed here, the Malacca Straits. Here you have a very narrow canal, a very narrow region, which currently carries something on the order of one-fifth of the entire world's trade. Not just for this region: If you take the entirety of world trade, something on the order of one-fifth goes through these narrow straits.

If you bring up the second graphic **(Figure 2)**, you can get a sense of the scale of this. This was from a 2013 video production by the LaRouche PAC, which you can find linked to the video description here. It's entitled *"The Kra Canal and the Development of Southeast Asia."*

In this graphic from that video, you can see that through these Straits of Malacca, which we just saw in the previous map, in 2012, for a representative year, you had something like 90,000 ships traveling through those straits, which was around three times the combined number of ships that traveled through the Panama Canal and the Suez Canal.

So the Panama and Suez Canals combined, times three, is the number of ships passing through the Straits of Malacca. And at the time of our production of this video, it was estimated that the traffic through the Malacca Straits was going to be increasing by about 20% each year, putting it on a direction to rather soon reach a maximum capacity. You can only fit so many ships through this region. And it's also relatively shallow, making it difficult for larger ships to even be able to get through this region at all.[1]

---

1. For further details on the limitations of the Straits and the proposed dimensions of the Kra Canal, see *The New Silk Road Becomes the World Land-Bridge*, a Special Report by *EIR*.

FIGURE 2

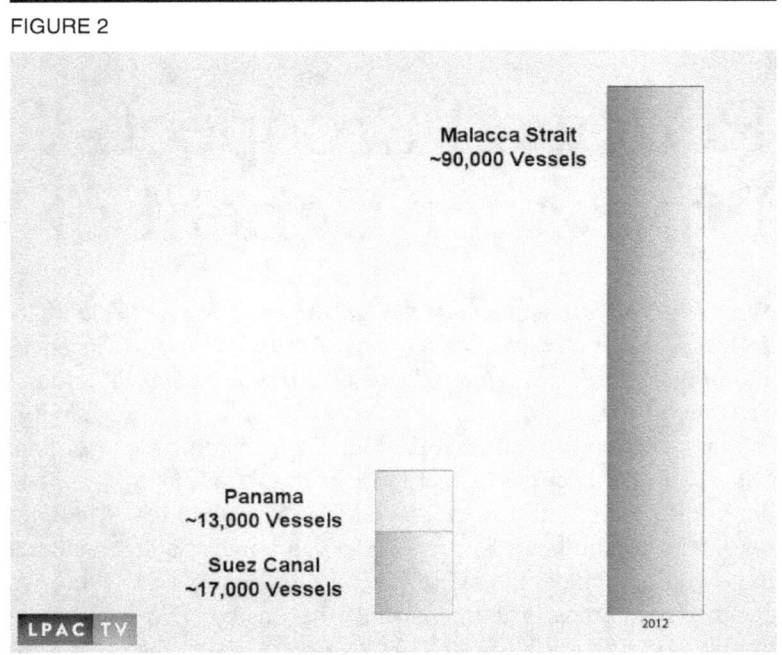

Malacca Bottleneck

It has been long known that this particular point in Southeast Asia, these Straits of Malacca, is a critical bottleneck for world trade, and world development. If you're going from East Asia to India, you've got to pass through this region. If you're going from East Asia into the Mediterranean, you have to pass through this region. If you want to go from East Asia into Europe, to the Atlantic on this route, you have to pass through this particular region.

This clearly becomes a major strategic choke point as well, vulnerable to sabotage through piracy, terrorism, or intention in a time of war.

There's been a long-standing proposal to develop a new shipping route, a new canal through Thailand, through the Kra Isthmus, and you can see this on the third graphic **(Figure 3)** displayed here. Again, a screen shot from our video, which presents this entire project, and its history in greater detail. Now you can see the path running through this rather narrow isthmus, through Thailand, through the Kra Isthmus.

Here we have the proposal to make this canal, which would cut out the need to go through these Straits of Malacca. This would cut off something like 1,000 miles from the trip, from the South China Sea into the Indian Ocean—not a huge, but a modest reduction in the actual distance traveled. Not the biggest in the world, but something certainly significant.

FIGURE 3

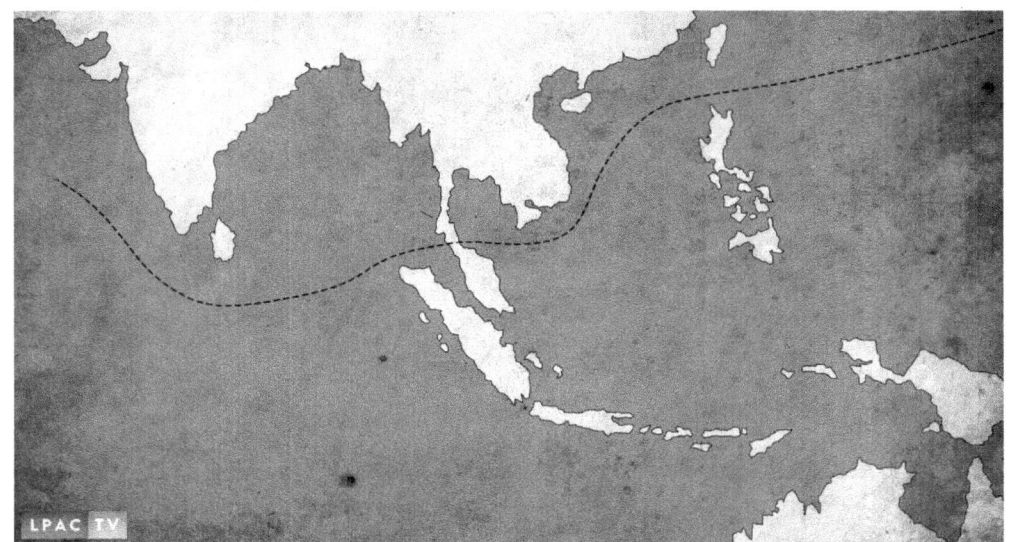

But probably more important than the distance, is that this would be a keystone project in just alleviating this bottleneck for this whole region, and being able to rapidly expand trade, and facilitate the continued expansion of trade through the Maritime Silk Road, from the developments in Asia, East Asia, in particular, again over to India, and as you can see in the fourth graphic **(Figure 4)** here, if you pair this with the recent incredible developments with Egypt's development of the New Suez Canal, you have a completely new potential for economic linking between the Pacific Ocean, between China, Russia's eastern borders, South Korea, Japan, this entire region, through the Kra Canal to India, to the entire Indian Ocean, up through the New Suez Canal into the Mediterranean, into Southern Europe, and then into the Atlantic.

So we have a new picture of linking the entire Pacific and the Atlantic in a completely new way.

Again, I'd like to direct people to the feature video that we produced in 2013 on this subject, "The Kra Canal and the Development of Southeast Asia." You

FIGURE 4

can see this in graphic 5 **(Figure 5)**, which is just an advertisement for the video.

FIGURE 5

This project has a long and important history, first conceived in the Seventeenth Century, with specific designs going back to the 1970s and earlier. In particular, we should note Mr. LaRouche's important role directly in the early 1980s, with his Fusion Energy Foundation, and his *Executive Intelligence Review* magazine sponsoring, in collaboration with the government of Thailand and collaborators from Japan, a series of conferences dedicated to the development of Southeast Asia, to the building of the Kra Canal, which Mr. LaRouche himself attended.

Economic Value Versus Money

So it's only appropriate, given the shifting world economic dynamic towards China, towards the BRICS, that now we're seeing it come back up and being put back on the table, as a prospective development project now.

I'd just like to conclude by emphasizing that I think this is an excellent case study in the type of shift in thinking that we need in the United States now. The difference between this insanity of Wall Street, where people are panicked about defending money that doesn't mean anything, money that has no actual existence in terms of any actual physical activity in the real economy, a completely worthless speculative bubble versus what we're seeing with things like the prospect for the Kra Canal, the construction of the Suez Canal.

We have new financial institutions being developed, such as the Asian Infrastructure Investment Bank, the North Asian Development Bank, the New Silk Road Development Bank, ready to create the credit to invest in these types of actual development projects. Projects that actually physically transform the physical economic potential of—as the case of the Kra Canal—not even of this entire region, but really of the whole world economy.

So, if you're going to reduce the time of trade through this region, if you're going to lower the physical costs, you're having a net physical impact on the entire world economy. You're lowering the physical costs of the goods, and in effect, you're raising the physical value provided to the entire world economy by those goods, by investing in these types of projects which can facilitate this whole process more efficiently.

It's a useful case study in the use of actual credit, a real credit system, to invest in real physical development, which actually has a measurable, understandable increase in the productive powers of the world economy: a measurable increase in the physical wealth, the lowering of the physical costs, increasing the physical wealth of the productive process of the entire world economy.

I think this is one among many critical lessons for what the United States needs to start doing, and thinking about, in a post-Wall Street era. And this should remind us of what we used to do, what we did under Franklin Roosevelt, of the types of real physical investment policies which contribute to creating a higher order future for our country for the coming generations. And this is absolutely what we need today.

I think that Mr. LaRouche's remarks about emphasizing the Kra Canal are an incredibly important and exciting keystone development for this entire perspective. This project gives us, again, another resounding clear message of where the rest of the world is going in creating a new economy, a new economic stage, a new higher-order future for their societies. This is just another message for the United States to get away from the control of Wall Street, and get serious, and participate in this type of development, these types of projects.

Italy: Development of the Mezzogiorno Is Back on the Agenda

by Claudio Celani

Sept. 18—The opening of the New Suez Canal, the refugee crisis in the Mediterranean, and a report last July on the decline of Southern Italy, in combination, have shaken up Italian politics and public opinion, creating a new awareness of the need—and the possibility—for a crash economic program to face the crises. We are still below the threshold, however, of a political decision to mobilize the necessary resources to do the job, which would mean breaking the chains of the current Euro system.

At the end of July, Svimez, a government-sponsored think-tank for the industrial development of Italy's Mezzogiorno, published its yearly report, which acknowledged that Southern Italy is facing industrial desertification and demographic annihilation. Measured in GDP, in the 2001-2014 period the Mezzogiorno declined faster than Greece: -9.4% against -1.7%. GDP growth has been negative for seven years in a row. Although all Italian regions have been hit by the economic collapse during 2008-2014, Southern Italy has lost cumulatively 13%, while Central/Northern Italy has lost "only" 7.4%.

The industrial collapse is more dramatic: Value added has collapsed by 45% in the Mezzogiorno, against 17.2% in the rest of the country. Building construction collapsed by 38.7% (vs. 29.8%).

This has produced an unprecedented, negative demographic trend. There were only 174,000 births in the Mezzogiorno region in 2014, in a population of 20.6 million. That is the lowest figure since the birth of the Italian state in 1862.

"Southern Italy will thus be characterized in the next years by a demographic distortion, a tsunami with unpredictable consequences, destined to lose 4.2 million inhabitants in the next 50 years," says Svimez.

The report, traditionally presented to all major state authorities and institutions, triggered a shock wave.

Courtesy of Movisol

Schiller Institute representative Massimo Lodi Rizzini addresses a Sept. 11 meeting of the Italian Democratic Party on developing the Mezzogiorno. Right from Rizzini are Massimo Guarascio of the University of Rome, and Enzo Siviero, University of Venice.

Seventy Democratic Party legislators signed a letter asking Prime Minister Matteo Renzi to address the issue. Pressure on Renzi is coming from below, as all Southern Italian regional administrations are ruled by his Democratic Party (DP), and all southern governors are united in demanding an investment plan.

Calabria Governor Mario Oliverio reported, "In the aftermath of the National DP Leadership meeting on August 7, finally the spotlights have been turned on and the debate has started again. Never has so much attention has been dedicated to ... the Mezzogiorno as now. This has not happened in 20 years." And his colleague Michele Emiliano, governor of the Apulia region, reminded Renzi that, "If we leave the Mezzogiorno to its fate, it will be a deadly threat to the country, but also a missed, irrecoverable opportunity."

The Suez Opportunity

The southern governors are well aware of the unique opportunity offered to the Southern Italian economy by the development around the "One Road and One Belt"

FIGURE 1

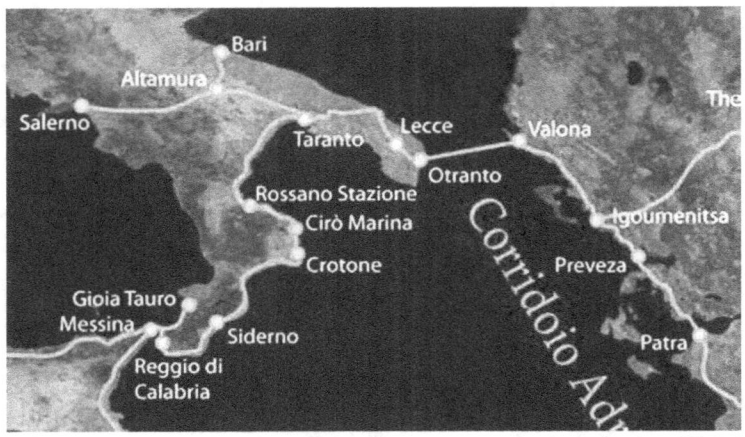

Courtesy of Movisol

Italy's Mezzogiorno, with key cities and proposed new transportation links highlighted. In the bottom left corner, the proposed Messina Bridge link to Sicily is shown; on the right, a proposed bridge across the Adriatic to Albania.

strategy of China and the BRICS countries as a whole. This became evident with the second shock, the opening of the New Suez Canal.

"Suez, a challenge for Sicily and Calabria" was the headline of the Messina-based newspaper *La Gazzetta del Sud,* the premier daily in Calabria and the third largest in Sicily, on Aug. 6, when Egypt's major infrastructure project was inaugurated.

It emphasized: "This tired and distracted Italy should mark the date of Thursday, August 6, on the calendar: Egypt will inaugurate the 'new' Suez Canal. There are two good reasons to focus on what a future-oriented country has been able to accomplish: One reason is linked to our past, and the other one to scenarios which will become true in a few years."

The first Suez Canal was based on the design of Luigi Negrelli, an Austro-Italian engineer, and was celebrated with Giuseppe Verdi's *Aida* in 1870. "A triumph of the Italian genius and of the will of the Egyptian people," the *Gazzetta* recalled. Today, Negrelli and Verdi are no longer with us, but "Italy cannot miss the value of such a revolution."

"Has anyone understood that Sicily and Calabria could garner the fruits of the increased traffic in the Southern Mediterranean region? It is a pity that our island [Sicily] is not physically connected with the rest of Italy [by a bridge, ed.] and that Gioia Tauro [the port in Calabria, ed.] is not well served by rail. We need to change that quickly." (**Figure 1**)

"Southern Italy cannot ignore this revolution, born of the will of an entire people: Consider that when the government announced the project, the sale of EGP 6.5 billion [$934 million] in bonds was completed in just 8 days. Egyptians scrambled to finance the great challenge. Here at home, instead, we have plenty of No Tav [No High Speed Rail, ed.], No Bridge, No This, and No That—regardless of the validity of the projects.

"Is there another Italy, looking to the future and willing to play a role?"

Another Italy

A first answer to this question came on Sept. 11 in Rome, when an important meeting, organized by the Democratic Party, included in the morning session all governors of southern Italian regions, and in the afternoon, featured a panel of experts comprising a Schiller Institute representative and a group of fiercely pro-development fighters led by Prof. Enzo Siviero, who builds bridges and is himself a supporter of the Schiller Institute.

The speech by Schiller Institute representative Massimo Lodi Rizzini, which focussed on the importance of a credit system for infrastructure, and the development of the Mezzogiorno as part of the World Land-Bridge and the BRICS/New Silk Road policy, was very well received.

The BRICS, led by China, Lodi Rizzini said, are now implementing the program which Lyndon LaRouche and the Schiller Institute have been fighting for over the last 40 years.

"Historically and geographically," he said, "Italy is an ideal bridge for connecting Europe and Africa, and this bridge must be physically built to plan the joint development of the two continents, a development envisioned by Enrico Mattei, the great industrial leader who, 60 years ago, wanted to bring technological progress to Africa and to the Middle East. On behalf of Italy, Mattei went to build and not to loot." (**Figure 2**)

Apparently, the Renzi government is split into two factions: One, led by Finance Minister Gian Carlo Padoan, wants to use the little money available for tax cuts for firms in the Mezzogiorno, although such a measure has never worked in an underdeveloped area; the other wants to use the money to finance infrastructure.

Indeed, the Ministry for Infrastructure has dedicated

its 2014-2020 plan entirely to the Mezzogiorno. The government lists all of the projects that are essential for enabling the southern Italian economy to reverse the collapse described in the *Gazzetta del Sud*, but with a missing link—the bridge over the Strait of Messina, which would connect the toe of the Italian peninsula with Sicily. Without the bridge the entire plan becomes useless.

FIGURE 2

The island of Sicily, with proposed tunnel-bridge links to Italy (upper right), and to Tunisia in Africa (lower left).

However, in response to grassroots pressure, on Sept. 10 a cabinet member announced an initiative to put the bridge back on the agenda. Interior Minister Angelino Alfano declared that his party, the New Center-Right (NCD), will soon introduce a draft bill to re-start procedures for construction of the Messina Bridge. When presenting the program of his party for the Mezzogiorno Sept. 10, Alfano said, "It is inconceivable that the [future] high-speed rail will stop at Reggio Calabria" at the toe of the peninsula, and not extend to Sicily and the city of Palermo."

Alfano's statements were welcomed by Pietro Salini, head of the Salini-Impregilo consortium that had already begun construction when, in 2013, the Monti government cancelled the project on behalf of the European Central Bank's austerity program. The consortium is building some of the largest infrastructure in the world, including the Panama Canal upgrade and the Grand Ethiopian Renaissance Dam.

The Messina bridge is indispensable for bringing together the upgraded system of integrated port, railway, and road infrastructure of Sicily and the southern Italian peninsula.

Del Monaco's Vision

How the system could work was illustrated by former government adviser Andrea del Monaco, writing in the *Gazzetta del Sud* earlier this year. Del Monaco pushes for an integrated system of ports and rail connections to make Southern Italy "the logistical base for a new productive basin in the Mediterranean." Southern Italian ports and upgraded logistics and rail networks would become the pivot for sea trade between South East Asia, Europe, and North America, del Monaco writes. In addition, three large new cities would be created by the connections among existing urban centers in the regions of Sicily, Basilicata, and Calabria.

The ports of Gioia Tauro, Crotone, and Taranto, he writes, "are the only ports serving four markets, i.e., Central Europe, North America, North Africa, and the Middle East."

Currently, 75% of container traffic—between South East Asia and North America—goes through the Pacific. The remaining 25% passes through the Mediterranean and enters the most important European markets through North European ports. Today, the hub-and-spokes model regulates transport of manufactured goods: They are first loaded onto large ships (mother ships) and unloaded in a few large ports (hubs) along pendulum routes, i.e. itineraries that connect the economically most important ports; in the second phase, goods are reloaded onto smaller ships (feeder ships) and delivered to their destinations (spokes).

Given the ever-larger size of ships and a the more and more frequent service demanded by their customers, large ships risk being underutilized. Only ports serving many markets can guarantee that the large ships will always be fully loaded. The southern Italian ports of Taranto, Gioia Tauro, and Crotone could be such ports, and would enable goods to reach Central Europe in five to seven days less than the current route through Gibraltar. Furthermore, large ships coming from Singapore, once they have unloaded/loaded freight with their origin/destination in Europe and in

FIGURE 3

Courtesy of Movisol

The three new "policentric" cities proposed by former government adviser Andrea del Monaco.

60 minutes. (**Figure 3**) These are the Messina-Reggio Calabria city created by the Messina Bridge; the "Apulo-Lucana City" (Potenza, Tricarico, Ferrandina, Matera, Altamura, Gravina, Genzano); and a third city, in Calabria (Cosenza, Scigliano, Serrastretta, Catanzaro).

This plan outlined by del Monaco is very similar to the one developed by this author in a series of LaRouche publications in 2012 under the headline "The Rebirth of Mezzogiorno." The critical issue is that under the current European Union system, it is not possible to generate credit to finance the project—or any other great project. A reorganization of the financial system and a Glass-Steagall banking separation regime is therefore urgent.

the Mediterranean, could continue to North America with less freight costs and more load.

"Taranto, Gioia Tauro, and Crotone would become the headquarters of world logistics, where the unloading/reloading of containers, assembly, collecting, and packaging of goods would be concentrated. Furthermore, their back-ports could become new production sites for shipyard and heavy machinery, dedicated to instrumental goods for steel, petrochemicals, building construction, and freight movement in port and railway terminals. The ports of Genoa and Trieste could specialize in receiving feeder ships with freight destined for Northern Europe" via land routes, says del Monaco.

Complementary to this logistics system, high-speed rail connections south of Salerno should not only be for passengers (350 kilometers per hour), but must become high capacity rail for both passengers and freight (250-300 kilometers per hour) and must connect five major population centers on the Italian mainland, and Messina and Palermo in Sicily.

Three new cities should be created through upgrading connections among existing population centers in an area where travellers could reach every point within

Every Day Counts In Today's Showdown To Save Civilization

That's why you need EIR's **Daily Alert Service**, a strategic overview compiled with the input of Lyndon LaRouche, and delivered to your email 5 days a week.

For example: On Sept. 30 EIR's Daily Alert featured Lyndon LaRouche's warning that the action must be taken immediately to remove President Obama in order to not only avoid further provocations toward World War III, but to avoid a disorderly collapse of Wall Street.

"If Wall Street collapses in a debt panic, that chaotic destructive force can lead to death and destruction in the United States and around the world," he said. FDR's Glass-Steagall is needed now.

Russian President Vladimir Putin's recent initiative in Syria has weakened Obama and created the necessary opening to do what's needed. But time is of the essence.

This is intelligence you need to act on, if we are going to survive as a nation and a species. Can you really afford to be without it?

THURSDAY, OCTOBER 1, 2015

EIR Daily Alert Service

EIR DAILY ALERT SERVICE P.O. BOX 17390, WASHINGTON, DC 20041-0390

- LaRouche: Wall Street Must Be Shut Down Before It Crashes
- Kerry Confirms Shift in U.S. Policy on Syria, Assad
- Putin Orders First Air Strikes Against Syrian Jihadists
- Russia's Upper House Approves Use of Armed Forces Abroad
- German Government Rejects Turkish Proposal for 'Safe Zones' in Syria
- Senator Warren: Glass-Steagall 'Is Exactly What We Should Do'
- German Saving Banks Threatened by Zero Rates Policy and EU Over-Regulation
- Senator Feinstein Thinks Russia's Move in Syria May Be Positive
- Dana Rohrabacher, Chair, House Subcommittee on Europe, Eurasia, and Emerging Threats, Holds Hearing on Terrorist Threat in Russia
- Rep. Dana Rohrabacher Attacks U.S. Support of Saudis, and Campaign To Overthrow Assad in House Foreign Affairs Committee
- BRICS Foreign Ministers Meet in New York
- NASA May Join Chinese/European Space Science Mission
- Finding Water on Mars Provokes Broad Debate in China
- Secretary John Kerry Reviews the 2013 Powerful Example of Cooperating with

---

✂

The 25th Amendment, Then and Now

by Theodore Andromidas

Sept. 21—On October 6th, 2010, less than two years after Barack Obama assumes office, speaking on the LPAC-TV *Weekly Report*, Lyndon LaRouche called for President Obama's immediate removal from office. For LaRouche it was clear, even this early in Obama's administration, that Obama was clearly no longer mentally competent to remain in that position of great command. LaRouche demanded the immediate invocation of the 25th Amendment, which provides for the orderly removal of a President, and his replacement by the Vice President, due to physical or mental impairment. "It requires no offense," LaRouche said, "other than the fact that he has got the [psychological—ed.] problems …

Generals Douglas MacArthur (left) and Dwight D. Eisenhower on a visit to Tokyo in May 1946. Both generals opposed Truman's decision to use the bomb in Japan.

that are diagnosed in fact, by Jerrold Post[1] and company who composed a study on the amendment."

For the second time since its ratification in 1967, the 25th Amendment is required to save our nation, and most of the world, from the threat of a deranged U.S. president, whose finger rests on the nuclear button. It was first used to remove a president certainly as corrupt, yet not, perhaps, as insane, as Obama—Richard Nixon.

The nation had survived 190 years, despite the illnesses of James Garfield, Woodrow Wilson, Franklin Roosevelt, and Dwight Eisenhower, without such a provision. However, since the passage of the 25th

Amendment in 1967, it has had much use. Why? In great part because the United States, in the aftermath of World War II, had assumed super-power status, and the deployment of nuclear weapons under the sole control of the President, requires that presidential succession be resolved in a swift and rational manner. This question of a swift succession, based on a review of the President's ability to carry out the duties of his office, became more critical than any time before 1945, in part, because of the new dangers posed by the emergence of the seemingly ever-present threat of nuclear war.

Harry Truman, Mass Murderer

These dangers clearly emerged first under the Truman Administration, when he ordered the nuclear annihilation of the Japanese cities of Hiroshima and

---

1. Jerrold Post. *The White House Years: Mandate for Change: 1953-1956: A Personal Account*, (New York: Doubleday, 1963), pp. 312-313.

Nagasaki, peddling the lie that it would "… save millions of American lives." This dangerous lie, that has outlived Truman, continues to this day.

> …President Harry Truman's decision to use the atomic bombs against Japan almost certainly saved lives. This is undoubtedly true if one accepts the arguments of U.S. leaders at the time; namely, that not using the atomic bomb would have forced the U.S. to launch a full invasion of Japan's home islands, and this would have killed far more people than Hiroshima and Nagasaki.[2]

Yet, it has been documented with certainty that there was almost universal opposition to the use of nuclear weapons against the Japanese homeland among "U.S. leaders" at the time, and most certainly from within our nation's *military* leadership. As can be seen by the following statements of two of the most important American generals of World War II, no military leader proposed or endorsed this insane, genocidal act as a way of shortening the war against Japan, or saving a million soldiers in an invasion of the Japanese homeland. General Dwight D. Eisenhower would later report:

> In 1945 … Secretary of War Stimson visited my headquarters in Germany, and informed me that our government was preparing to drop an atomic bomb on Japan. I was one of those who felt that there were a number of cogent reasons to question the wisdom of such an act…. I voiced to him my grave misgivings, first on the basis of my belief that Japan was already defeated and that dropping the bomb was completely unnecessary and second because I thought that our country should avoid shocking world opinion by the use of a weapon whose employment was, I thought, no longer mandatory as a measure to save American lives.[3]

In 1985 Richard Nixon would recall discussing the bombings of Hiroshima and Nagasaki with General of the Army Douglas MacArthur:

> MacArthur once spoke to me very eloquently about it, pacing the floor of his apartment in the Waldorf. He thought it a tragedy the bomb was ever exploded. MacArthur believed that the same restrictions ought to apply to atomic weapons as to conventional weapons, that the military objective should always be limited damage to noncombatants … MacArthur, you see, was a soldier. He believed in using force only against military targets, and that is why the nuclear thing turned him off, which I think speaks well of him.[4]

Other senior U.S. military leaders disagreed with the necessity of the nuclear bombings of Japan. These included Fleet Admiral William Leahy, Chief of Staff to the President; Brigadier General Carter Clarke, the military intelligence officer who prepared intercepted Japanese cables for U.S. officials; Fleet Admiral Chester Nimitz, Commander in Chief of the Pacific Fleet; and even the man in charge of all strategic air operations against the Japanese home islands, then-Major General Curtis LeMay. But the actual reason for Truman's decision to use the A-bomb was in fact, as Eisenhower warned, for the sake of "shocking world opinion."

After these two horrific acts of mass murder by a United States President, Truman would be president for another seven years, repeatedly threatening to bring the world to the brink of nuclear annihilation. In 1948, Truman once again put his finger on the nuclear button, this time in Europe. During the Berlin Blockade of 1948-49, Truman transferred B-29 bombers capable of delivering nuclear bombs to the European region as a signal to the Soviet Union—in the days before the USSR had developed nuclear weapons—that the United States was both capable of implementing a nuclear attack, and willing to execute it.

During the Korean War Truman brought the world to the 'brink' once again, deploying the B-29s to signal U.S. resolve. The use of nuclear weapons was openly discussed as the means of reversing U.S. setbacks and losses during the Korean War. One of the pervasive and pernicious lies of the Korean conflict is that Truman fired MacArthur because MacArthur wanted to drop "the bomb" on North Korea. Not only did MacArthur not advocate the use of nuclear weapons to re-

2. Gar Alperovitz, *The Decision to Use the Atomic Bomb and the Architecture of an American Myth* (New York: Knopf, 1995).
3. *Military Situation in the Far East*, Hearings, 82d Congress, 1st Session, Part 1, p. 77.
4. James Carroll, "Nixon's madman strategy," *Boston Globe*, June 14, 2005.

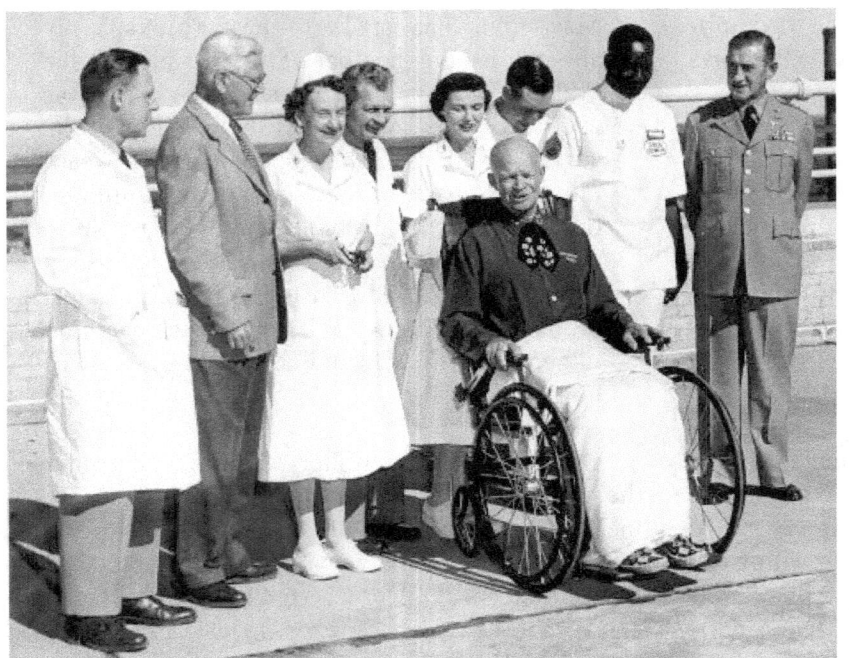

President Dwight Eisenhower, in his first public appearance after suffering a heart attack on October 25, 1955.

transfer of temporary or, if necessary, permanent powers from the President to Vice President, was signed by both men. But many considered this approach an inadequate solution, since it left the decision solely in the hands of the President and Vice President. Therefore two senators introduced legislation to deal with those inadequacies: New Deal Democrat Estes Kefauver of Tennessee and Democratic Senator Birch Bayh of Indiana.

Following Eisenhower's stroke in 1957, Kefauver, who had been the 1956 Democratic Party nominee for Vice President, opened hearings before the Senate's Subcommittee on Constitutional Amendments. He presented a proposal similar to the disability agreement between Eisenhower and Nixon, but included modifications designed to address those concerns expressed by some members of Congress.

cover the situation, but in public testimony before a Senate inquiry, he said that he had never recommended their use. In 1960, MacArthur challenged a statement by Truman that he [MacArthur] had wanted to use nuclear weapons. Truman was forced to issue a retraction, stating that he had no documentary evidence for this claim; it was merely his, Truman's, personal opinion.

It became clear to many in various positions of authority, that a clear chain of succession for the presidency, if and when the President were not capable of sane and rational decision, would be essential, perhaps even to the future of Humanity.

Senator Estes Kefauver—The Kefauver Plan

Once again, contrary to common belief, what was to become the 25th Amendment was not introduced as a result of the assassination of President John Kennedy. Rather it was President Dwight Eisenhower's 1955 heart attack and subsequent health problems over the next two years, that put the question of presidential disability and succession in the minds of much of the leadership of the nation. In what perhaps was an example of profound prescience, it was not just a question of how, but *who* was to succeed the President. In 1957, the Eisenhower-Nixon letter of agreement, working out the

Those concerns centered on the absence of any means of settling a dispute between a President and Vice President over the state of the President's health. This was an absolutely critical question for the nation, especially with Richard Nixon as Vice President. It was clear to many—especially to Kefauver, who had not just been not a political opponent but was also Nixon's next door neighbor in Washington—that the issue of succession should not be left in the hands of a man many knew to be an unprincipled political opportunist.

The original Kefauver proposal, presented in 1958, called for the Vice President and a majority of the members of the cabinet to present the issue before Congress, whereupon the Congress would decide the matter—a two-thirds vote of each house being necessary to declare the President incapable of continuing in office. Kefauver ultimately recommended a constitutional amendment that, unlike the Eisenhower-Nixon Agreement, did not establish a specific procedure, but rather gave Congress the general power to establish, by law, a procedure by which it could declare a President disabled.

With President John F. Kennedy's assassination, the need for a clear way to determine presidential succession—especially with the new reality of a possible nuclear Armageddon—forced Congress to act. The new

President, Lyndon B. Johnson, had once suffered a heart attack, and the next two people in line for the Presidency were Speaker of the House John McCormack, who was 71 years old, and Senate President *pro tempore* Carl Hayden, who was 86 years old. This time it was Senator Birch Bayh, who had succeeded Kefauver as Chairman of the Subcommittee on Constitutional Amendments, who began to advocate a detailed amendment on presidential succession. Adopted first by Nebraska on July 12, 1965, the Amendment was certified on February 23, 1967.

There are four crucial sections to the 25th Amendment:

Section 1: The process by which the Vice President becomes President if the current President dies, resigns, or is removed from office.

President Richard Nixon, proponent of the "Madman Doctrine."

Section 2: If the Vice Presidency becomes vacant, the President may choose a new Vice President, who must be voted on and approved by Congress.

Section 3: The President may temporarily make the Vice President the Acting President with a written declaration that endures until a second declaration ends this condition.

But most important for the nation—then under Nixon, and now with Obama—is:

Section 4: This is an emergency provision that allows the Vice President and a majority of the Cabinet to declare the President unfit to carry out the duties of the Presidency. The President may assert his competency (ability to serve) by sending a declaration to Congress. The Vice President and Cabinet can submit another declaration of the unfitness of the President, which would force Congress to reach a two-thirds majority vote that the President is unfit for office.

Although Section 4 has never *formally* been used, it was used *de facto* in the removal of one of the most insane presidents in our history.

Richard Nixon—The Madman Theory

On August 22, 1974, less than two weeks after his resignation, and less than a month after articles of impeachment against President Richard Nixon had passed the House Judiciary Committee, *The Washington Post* printed a short, hardly noticeable, article. It was entitled "Pentagon Kept Watch on Military."

This relatively innocuous headline actually concealed explosive allegations. It reported that during the final days of the Nixon Administration, Defense Secretary James Schlesinger and the Joint Chiefs of Staff had "... kept a close watch to make certain that no orders were given to military units outside the normal chain of command." The article asserted that this extraordinary alert was only "... based on hypothetical situations that *could* [emphasis added] arise during a period when President Nixon's hold on the presidency" and his sanity "... was not clear." Pentagon sources also said, according to the article, that no one had any evidence that any such action was being contemplated, but steps were taken to ensure that no military commander would take an order from the White House or anywhere else that did not come through military channels.

But even before the 1968 presidential election, Nixon would demonstrate the quality of corrupt insanity that led to his removal from office six years later. *Politico*, a Capitol Hill newspaper, reported one important instance in a June 9, 2014 article by John Aloysius Farrell, entitled, "Yes, Nixon Scuttled the Vietnam Peace Talks." Nixon aide Tom Charles Huston had prepared a comprehensive, still-secret report, which said that Johnson would try to help the Democratic nominee—Vice President Hubert Humphrey—by staging an October surprise. When LBJ announced to the nation, just days before the balloting, that he was calling a halt in the bombing of North Vietnam to help fuel progress in ongoing peace talks, a paranoid Nixon was sure that his fears had been realized.

Anna Chennault, a Republican activist with ties to the South Vietnamese government, sent word to Saigon that it would get better terms if Humphrey lost and Nixon took office, the FBI would discover.[5]

From literally his first days in office, Nixon placed the world on the edge of a nuclear precipice. To lead his inner circle of advisers, Nixon promoted the man who would become the model for Stanley Kubrick's Cold War classic character in the movie, *Dr. Strangelove or: How I Learned to Stop Worrying and Love the Bomb,* Henry Kissinger. Nixon and Kissinger then launched a new military initiative: "The Madman Theory."

Nixon explained this new strategy to his White House Chief of Staff, H.R. Haldeman:

> I call it the Madman Theory, Bob. I want the North Vietnamese to believe I've reached the point where I might do anything to stop the war. We'll just slip the word to them that, "for God's sake, you know Nixon is obsessed about communism. We can't restrain him when he's angry—and he has his hand on the nuclear button" and Ho Chi Minh himself will be in Paris in two days begging for peace.[6]

In October 1969, the Nixon Administration warned that "the madman was loose" when the United States military was ordered to full global war readiness alert (of which the American population was completely unaware), and bombers armed with thermonuclear weapons flew patterns near the Soviet border for three consecutive days.

Nixon and Kissinger used the madman strategy sev-

Today's candidate for the 25th Amendment, President Barack Obama.

eral other times in the following years. It was reported that the "madman strategy" was used to force the North Vietnamese to the peace table. It has also been reported that Henry Kissinger, and others, would portray the 1970 Cambodian Campaign as a symptom of Nixon's lunacy.

Actual Lunacy

In fact, actual lunacy seems to have been at the very core of Nixon and Kissinger's thinking. In his *Secrets: A Memoir of Vietnam and the Pentagon Papers,* Daniel Ellsberg reports the following discussion:

> Nixon: I still think we ought to take the North Vietnamese dikes out now. Will that drown people?
>
> Kissinger: About two hundred thousand people.
>
> Nixon: No, no, no, I'd rather use the nuclear bomb. Have you got that, Henry?
>
> Kissinger: That, I think, would just be too much.
>
> Nixon: The nuclear bomb, does that bother you? I just want you to think big, Henry, for Christsakes.[7]

The Watergate scandal began with a burglary at the

---

5. Robert D. Schulzinger, *U.S. Diplomacy Since 1900*, (Oxford University Press, 2002), p. 303.
6. Michael S. Sherry, *In the Shadow of War*, (Yale University Press, 1995), p. 312.

7. Daniel Ellsberg, *Secrets: A Memoir of Vietnam and the Pentagon Papers* (Penguin, 2003), p.418.

Watergate Hotel in June 1972 and ended with a President's resignation in August 1974. The move to clean out the Nixon Presidency began in January 1973, when Senator Ted Kennedy (D-Mass.) introduced a resolution to establish a Select Committee on Presidential Campaign Activities to investigate campaign activities related to the presidential election of 1972. In October 1973, Vice President Spiro Agnew resigned, to be replaced—according to the Constitutional procedures established by the 25th Amendment—by then-Senate Minority leader Gerald Ford. Nixon would go next.

There were three options: Senate impeachment, which was a certainty; invoking the 25th Amendment, which was under active consideration and in process; and Nixon's resignation. Although Section 4 of the 25th Amendment was never publicly invoked, both Secretary of Defense Schlesinger and White House Chief of Staff Alexander Haig based themselves on Section 4 when they told the Joint Chiefs not to act on any Nixon order without first checking with them, according to qualified *EIR* sources. In August 1974, Nixon resigned and, once again under the terms of the 25th Amend-

ment, Gerald Ford became the 38th President of the United States. The great danger of a corrupt and lunatic presidency had, for the time being, been averted.

Today, as then, the President of the United States himself represents the greatest threat to the future of our nation and all humanity. This threat has been repeatedly and exhaustively documented in the pages of *Executive Intelligence Review.*

Five years have passed since Lyndon LaRouche provided that clinical assessment of a deranged President and named the methods available for his removal. In these five years we have moved closer and closer to nuclear conflict once again. We have seen an insane expansion of wars from the Ukraine in Eastern Europe to islands in the South China Sea.

And yet, in these same five years, we have seen President Putin, President Xi, and the leadership of the BRICS nations create the conditions for lasting peace and economic development on the planet. The 25th Amendment was created, and adopted, to deal with just the kind of threat we face today, a deranged President, Barack Obama, occupying the White House. It must be invoked once again.

The Harmony of Mental Spheres: 'God's Brain,' William Warfield's Mind

by Dennis H. Speed

(Music) is that part of us that is connected with the Divine One. I remember Dr. Thurman once said, God created man in His own image in the dead center, so that in the dead center of God's brain, there is this image of what man *is*; and at a point at which man reaches the full development of that image, then he will be on a par with the angels.... And I never forgot that: "Ah! So that's what evolution is about! Man finally coming *into the image* that is in the dead center of God's brain, of what man *is to be*!... And all of us are endowed with that basic thing, and *Music is it*.

> William Warfield, interview
> with *Fidelio*, November 1994

Sept. 20—When baritone William Warfield (1920-2002), later a board member of the Schiller Institute, first met its representatives at a conference of the National Association of Negro Musicians in 1993, he autographed a copy of his autobiography *My Music And My Life*: "Sincere regards, and keep up the fight (for) A=430." That was Warfield, known affectionately by his students as "Uncle Bill." He could appear easy-going, but would always admonish anyone whom he thought had talent, in any field, emphasizing that it was above all a fierce, untiring, single-minded focus on the musician's art, or in the chosen profession, that must always come first. As his friend and fellow Institute board member Sylvia

EIRNS/Stuart Lewis

William Warfield performing at the Schiller Institute conference in February 2002, the year of his death.

Olden Lee would say, "It is necessary that one deserve perfection, in order to achieve perfection."

A year later, in May 1994, Warfield would collaborate, together with baritone Robert McFerrin, tenor George Shirley, and accompanist Sylvia Lee on behalf of the Schiller Institute's National Conservatory of Music Movement at a day-long seminar and evening concert at Howard University in Washington, D.C. Both Warfield and Lyndon LaRouche spoke at that seminar, and it was there that they met for the first time. From that time until Warfield's death nine years later, the two remained "dialogue partners" and friends (see LaRouche's remarks about Warfield in this issue).

Youthful Preparation

LaRouche and Warfield were both World War Two veterans, each of whom would discover the missions they would devote the rest of their lives to through the fiery crucible of that conflict. Warfield had a way throughout his life of turning every seeming disadvantage into the very means that propelled him forward, often inadvertently accomplishing unintended good in the process. For example, there was the time that, as a 17-year old, he unintentionally integrated a St. Louis hotel as the "dark horse" winner of the National Music Educators League competition. As he recounted in his autobiography:

There were several of us

from Rochester who went to the regional, and several of the regional finalists went to the national in St. Louis in the Spring of 1938. Rochester's showing was the best case that could be made for the quality of music education in our school system. One of my close friends, Anthony Giardino, made the first cut with me... The only discomfort I felt, when I took first prize, was that I had beaten out Tony.

The prize gave me the option of attending a number of music schools, including Julliard... I was the only black singer in the local or regional competitions. I don't believe there were any other singers in the national either, because I was told that I had later inadvertently desegregated the Jefferson Hotel in St. Louis by becoming the first black guest ever to be registered there. My reservation was made in advance along with the other finalists. I suppose they never imagined that any of them would be African-Americans.

By age 21, thanks to his work with dedicated teachers at the University of Rochester's Eastman School of Music, as well as excellent preparation gained at Washington High School, Warfield was fluent in German, Italian, and French. He had also accumulated a hefty repertoire of English-language accents which would stand him in good stead in the "radio days" of the late 1940s and 1950s. Recordings from that period testify to his formidable command of diction, projection, intonation, delivery, and, most importantly, communication of the intent of a song.

This extraordinary skill was particularly useful to him in his job an an intelligence officer during the Second World War. Part of a unit charged with preparing seven-man intelligence units for missions in Europe, on occasion Warfield encountered German POWs. Others marveled at Warfield's ability to gain the confidence of these men, by simply singing Schubert and Brahms lieder for them, or with them, as the case might be, after which they freely shared information which they were severely reluctant to give to "hard cop" interrogators.

Unrelenting Dedication

Warfield wrote in his autobiography:

It was becoming clearer all the time that when

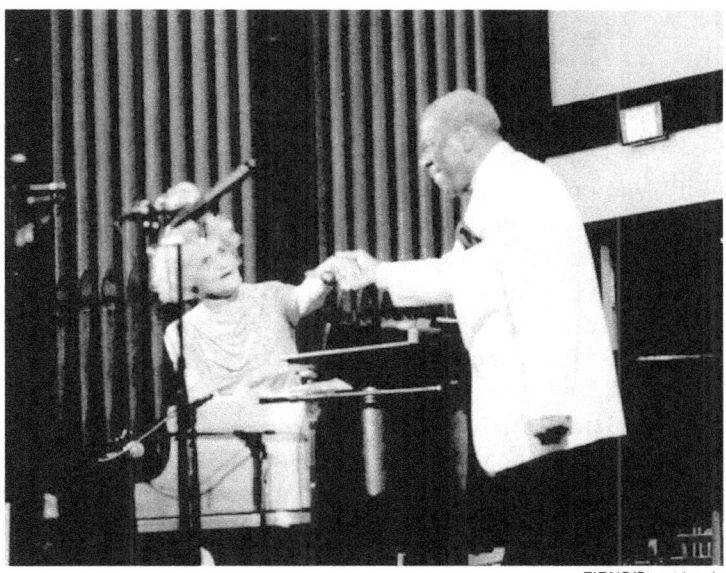

EIRNS/Stuart Lewis

William Warfield and Silvia Olden Lee, after their performance at Howard University Rankin Memorial Chapel in May of 1994.

the war ended and my military service was through I would be stepping out into a no-man's land. There simply was no career ladder for a black classical singer. The opera world wasn't ready for me or any other black male. Hollywood, too, offered only stereotypes for the most part, and the situation was the same for mainstream Broadway theater. The concert world was all there was, it seemed, and that was shaky, at best.

In that five-sentence summary is contained almost a century of injustice and American cultural self-sabotage. While the Fisk Jubilee Singers enjoyed some popularity in the United States (and more in Europe) during the 1870s and 1880s, even composer Antonin Dvořák could not convince the Metropolitan Opera to allow African-Americans, such as the great Sissieretta Jones, to sing on its stage in the 1890s. (In 1892, Jones became the first African-American to perform in Carnegie Hall, and worked with Dvořák when Dvořák lived in New York City in 1893 and 1894.)

Warfield's fellow Schiller Institute board member and sometimes accompanist, renowned vocal coach Sylvia Olden Lee, never tired of pointing out that her very mother had been offered a lead role in a Puccini opera debut at the Metropolitan Opera, if she would "pass for white" and live a separate life, pretending not to be married to her darker-skinned, obviously African-

American husband. (Sylvia Lee, as the first African-American vocal coach at the Met, would be responsible for the Met hiring Marian Anderson to sing there in 1955—six decades after Dvořak's work with violinist Will Marion Cook, soprano Sissieretta Jones, and singer, arranger, and composer Harry Burliegh, one of Warfield's heroes.)

Lyndon LaRouche recently emphasized, including on the occasion of his own 93rd birthday, that the injustice that was faced by, and overcome by those of Warfield's and earlier generations, in their not being allowed to perform on the opera stage, cannot be separated, either from the terrible legacy of the Confederate system—a system that has taken over the Presidency today in the form of the Cheney/Bush and Obama Administrations—or from the wholesale destruction of American education that has occurred since the 1890s, and became hegemonic in 1900 through the work of Bertrand Russell, John Dewey and others.

The music and languag-study curriculum that was available to Warfield in high school in the 1930s is virtually unavailable in nearly any American public high school today, and certainly to the population of such cities as Warfield's own Rochester, New York. The popular culture that began its descent into hell in 1913 with Stravinsky's *Rite of Spring* ritual murder of beauty, has resulted in cultural tone-deafness. That is the reason our population cannot discern, or, even worse, chooses not to discern that there is *no* distinction between the bellowing of a Donald Trump, the hissing of a Dick Cheney, the snarling of a Barack Obama, or the braying of a Bush "43."

Were our civilization to survive, the prohibition of the discovery by a child of the idea of harmony, is what is necessary to reverse. Our moral elevation and progressive evolution in a thermonuclear age, to become capable of carrying out the mission for which mankind is designed by subsuming the dissonance of inferior non-human expressions of speech and music, requires that unrelenting dedication to the mission of mankind—universal harmony—that William Warfield exemplified. He was humanity at its best, transcending widespread injustice and adversity through a far more universal musical harmony of the soul.

Where is the dead center of the mind of God? It is everywhere; its circumference, nowhere. "All of us are endowed with that basic thing, and *Music is it!*"

Dr. William Warfield, Baritone

'Music Is the Kingdom of Heaven, Education Is the Kingdom of Heaven'

This is an excerpt from an interview with Dr. William Warfield by Dennis and Lynne Speed, done in November 1994, and published in Fall 1995 issue of the Schiller Institute's Fidelio *magazine.*

Fidelio: When you did your first concert at Town Hall in New York City, I understand that one of the things you did that was groundbreaking at the time, was to include a Spiritual at the top of the program, rather than putting them at the end.

I believe that you did a comparison between the spiritual "A City Called Heaven" and, I believe, a Twelfth-century—.

William Warfield: Yes, Thirteenth Century, a *Conductus,* it is called.

Someone asked me about that last night, because they said, "Well, you know, Mr. Warfield, I was of the impression that Paul Robeson had done that with his program, and started off with Spirituals," which was before me, and I said, "Yes."

The difference was this. The Classical format is to start out with the Baroque period, in which you have Handel and Bach, and pre-Handel, and all of that. And then you have a group of *lieder,* in which you do the Schubert, Schumann, Brahms, and all of that. And then, in the middle of the program, there's usually an opera aria, which is usually in Italian. Then you come back and you do America, and you end up with Spirituals—*if* you were Black, you ended with Spirituals; not necessarily everybody did that. But it was usually something that was native or belonged to the United States, or something like that.

Now, what I did was this. I decided that I wanted to make the first group a religious group, and I called it, "Songs of the Believer." And in that group, I put Schütz's "Eile mich Gott zu erretten," which was German, pre-Bach; I went back and got a little *Conduc-*

tus of Perotin, who was the organist at Notre Dame back in the Thirteenth Century. I got a *Kol Nidre,* a Jewish arrangement of the *Kol Nidre,*—I don't remember who did it. I did a setting of the 150th Psalm by Monteverdi. And *in that group,* I put a traditional American Negro Spiritual. *That* was what was different, the fact that I programmed that in the first group, with all of these other things.

And the reason I did that, was this. We were speaking of the internationality of music, and back in the Thirteenth Century, in Latin, Pérotin said [sings]: "Homo vidi que pro te passior si es dolor sicut, sicut cor passior . . . ."

And then you have [sings Spiritual]: "I am a poor pilgrim of sorrow, I've roamed through this wide world alone. . . ." That's the same thing, yet they're centuries apart. And that was what Sylvia was mentioning last night, she still talks about it. It was the first time anybody included a Spiritual, and it *matched* something that was written back in the Thirteenth Century.

Fidelio: We should just indicate that you're speaking of Sylvia Olden Lee, who is one of the great masters of the playing and arrangement of Spirituals.

I want to ask another question, while we're on the topic. You mentioned the spontaneous response you would get from people, and you've just shown us an example of the identity of the content of the music, despite the fact that the forms, or the languages, at least, may be somewhat different—the "clothing" may be a little bit different.

But could you say something also about what you think the work is that goes into this? For example, how one accurately delivers, declaims, a Spiritual, or another song? I know you've done a lot of work on different components of language, and how they directly contribute to doing a song well.

William Warfield: Let me say something about that, and then I would like to tell you about an experience I had once with Dr. Robert Nathaniel Dett, when I was a youngster. As you know, he got one of his degrees at the Eastman School of Music, and during that time, he formed a choir, and I was a teenager in Dr. Dett's choir. For instance, I learned "Listen to the Lambs"

EIRNS/Stuart Lewis

William Warfield and Lyndon LaRouche, at the podium for a panel discussion at the Howard University event in May 1994, entitled "For a Marian Anderson National Conservatory of Music Movement."

from him. I've done that so many times, and performed it with groups, I know exactly what he expected of it. And, the many times that I've conducted that with groups, I still do it just as Dr. Dett taught me.

But, basically, let me first say this. Number one, there is a *great deal* of learning and development one has to do with the voice as a technique, to know *how* to use the voice. Then, there's a great deal of *learning* one has to do with languages, so that if you're going to do *lieder* and opera and things like that, you know what you're doing. These are mechanical things that have to precede your being able to even utter a sound, if you're going to be in Classical music.

Now, once that is accomplished, and you know languages, and you know how to use your voice and it's strictly under your control, when it gets back to the projecting or the making of music, there's no difference in doing a Spiritual or a German *lied.* You learn all of the technique of *doing* languages and using your voice, but when it comes down to the so-called nitty-gritty in performing, the performance approach is the same.

I'll tell you why I discovered this, how I became aware of this. I was a youngster, I was about eighteen years old, and I did a radio show, and Dr. Dett listened to it, and I came to his studio the next day, and I said, "Dr. Dett, how was it?" and he said, "Young man, it was very fine, very fine. But what did *you* think about it? How did you think you did?" I had done a German piece, a French piece; I ended up with a Spiritual, and I started with Handel. And I said, "Well, of course, the Handel and things, I think that went very well. Of course there's nothing new to me with that, because we sing 'The Messiah' and all of that in church all the time. It was quite natural." And then I said, "People told me that my German was excellent, that my pronunciation was fine and that they liked this, they liked that, and the French song, my French teacher told me that the pronunciation was beautiful and I did everything right." And so on and so forth.

And he said, "What did you think about singing the Spirituals?" I said, "Oh, when I got to the Spirituals, I was at home." And he said, "Hhhmm. Young man, when you feel the same way about your German and your French, as you feel about that Spiritual, you'll be an artist."

I looked at him, and *boing!*, something went off in my head. And to this day, I can sing Schubert's "Wohin?," and tell all about the brook in German, and turn right around and sing a Spiritual, and there's basically *no* difference in making music, whether I do it in the Spiritual, or in the German *lied.*

And *that* is all a part of this thing I called the universality of music. That is when your spirit comes out, and your spirit shines. All right, I can sing in German, I can sing Italian. I can do this. But when it comes right down to it, if I am singing an aria, and want to sing "Heavenly Aida"—[sings] "Celeste Aida . . .,"—as the tenors do in *Aida,* it's the same thing as singing, "Didn't my Lord deliver Daniel?" *It's the same basic emotion.* You're expressing your emotion through music. And when you discover that, music is on such a plane that you can sit by yourself sometimes, and make yourself weak just singing—because it's coming out of you, it's part of you.

Fidelio: I've had the pleasure of seeing a few of your master classes with the youngsters who are learn-

William Warfield at a rehearsal by the Leesburg Schiller Institute chorus in May 1995.

ing to sing, and I know that you have emphasized to them a great deal, *what* they're saying, *what* they're communicating, getting across a point, and that they must utilize the prosody which is embedded in the language, be it English, or German, or French, to bring out the meaning, and make an artistic presentation. Perhaps you could give us an example of that. I know one wonderful thing you have done, is in some of the Spirituals that have a repeated phrase, where you need to really bring this out in certain ways.

William Warfield: Yes. This is also true with *anything.* In German, for instance, where you have phrase after phrase after phrase repeated, and verse after verse, as in Schubert sometimes—you know, in "Ungeduld," and things like that, the idea is to see that when you do something each time, it has a different emphasis, or a different accent, or expanding the thought. For instance, I have a lot of fun doing Margaret Bond's Spiritual, "Didn't It Rain?":

Children, didn't it rain?
Oh my Lord, didn't it, didn't it, didn't it?
Oh my Lord, didn't it rain?

And she does that all the way through. And I get a big kick out of seeing how many times I can say "Didn't it?" differently than the time before. There are so many possible ways you can say "didn't it, didn't it, didn't it"; and if every time you say "didn't it, didn't it, didn't it" in a monotonous way—well, I mean, get off that box! Do something with it! Get involved with "didn't it." See how many different ways you can say "didn't it?" It's that kind of thing.

And this is true with a little thing like, for instance, the "Wohin?" of Schubert, where he says,

Wohl aus dem Felsenquell . . .
Ich hört' ein Bächlein rauschen,
Wohl aus dem Felsenquell.

And then sometimes it's

Hinunter und immer weiter,
Und immer dem Bache nach,
Und immer frischer rauschte,
  [sings *forte*:]
Und immer frischer rauschte,
Und immer heller der Bach.

It's the same thing. He's repeating "und immer ..." and always it's fresh, and you hear the brook speaking louder, then you repeat that, and you say it differently. And this is to me the essence of your projecting and your making something of music. It's just not reading off something.

Yesterday, we had a wonderful session having to do with the Spiritual, and Sylvia came out after the students had done it, and then we got them to loosen up. And we said, "Let it all hang out." All right. This was "Swing Low, Sweet Chariot." [sings, *piano*:] "Swing Low, Sweet Chariot, comin' for to carry me home, Swing low, sweet chariot, comin' for to carry me home." Now the next time, [changes accent on words] "Oh, Swing low, sweet chariot [*forte*:] comin' for to carry me home, Oh, swing low, sweet chariot—."

All of that is possible, when you let yourself go, just let it come out as your expression of what you're saying, and not simply what's on the paper. "Now I'm going to do what *I* feel like I want to express in singing this." [sings] "I locked over Jordan and what did I see? [*piano*:] Comin' for to carry me home. Ohhhh, a band of angels comin' after me, [*forte*:] comin' for to carry me home." All of that, is my expression of what I feel about what I'm singing, and you're not going to find it on the paper.

This is what we were doing yesterday, and the audience just responded like crazy, because they recognized what was happening. Music was *expressing* itself, not just being sung.

Fidelio: I wanted to say about that experience yesterday, that what you hit on in your description, is what I'd call the essence of real education.

William Warfield: That's right. That's the whole thing.

Only a Fundamental Reversal of Economic Policy Can Solve the Refugee Crisis

by Helga Zepp-LaRouche, Chairman of the German political party, Büso

Sept. 22—In these stormy days in world politics there are two fundamentally different types of political and financial policy leaders: those guided by an optimistic image of man, who put forward a clear vision for the future of mankind, and those whose smallmindedness leaves no room for any image of man. Looking backward, they seek only to defend their power and evil deeds of the past—even though they are no longer defensible. In the dramatic changes of the coming weeks, we will only be able to solve the problems confronting us if we succeed in winning the European nations and the United States to the new paradigm represented by the economic policy of the BRICS states and the "win-win" perspective of China's New Silk Road.

There are signs of both tendencies in the refugee crisis, which is out of control in many EU countries, and exposes the lack of EU solidarity. After Chancellor Merkel, with her "We will do it!" had given a positive signal—in view of the unmanageable situation of so many refugees streaming into Greece, the Balkans, and Italy—Finance Minister Schäuble and Interior Minister de Maizière went straight into reverse. Schäuble, who is plagued by everything (except economic expertise), immediately repeated his mantra of a "zero deficit" in light of the initial costs of the admission of the refugees, and demanded cuts of an arbitrary sum of 500,000 Euros in other expenditures.

His approach showed the same underlying mentality of the taskmaster that we had seen in the brutal treatment of the Syriza government in Greece, and was probably intended to stir up the population, which had just shown generosity toward the refugees, against these same people, according to the motto: Either your daycare centers, or hostels for the refugees.

In contrast, however, and much more purposefully, several representatives of industry associations—from Ulrich Grillo of the Federation of German Industries to Ingo Kramer and Alexander Wilhelm of the Confederation of German Employer Associations—pointed to the great benefits of the immigration of workers for the German economy, in view of the 600,000 vacancies in the labor market. Wilhelm stressed that there are no signs that the refugees would take jobs away from anyone.

The positive aspect of the government's intention to spend two billion Euros for language classes to integrate the refugees is matched in the negative, as it were, by the 150-page draft law developed by de Maizière's Interior Ministry, designed for deterrence. It denies asylum seekers a decent minimum subsistence and replaces it with handouts of goods. For a large number of the asylum seekers, it will provide nothing a bag lunch and a rail ticket back to the country in which they first entered the EU. The authors of this catalog of measures obviously lack any understanding of the strategic situation, the human dimension, or the possibility of solving the crisis.

The EU presents a picture of great disunity, once again showing with unsurpassed clarity that there is no "European people," but merely a supranational oligarchical bureaucracy, which has hardly anything to offer, other than the inhuman Frontext border guard program for scaring away refugees, and rules which increasingly no one is following.

Glass-Steagall or Chaos

A change of scene. Last Thursday, the long-anticipated increase in interest rates by the Open Market Committee of the U.S. Federal Reserve Bank was once again postponed, and interest rates will therefore remain at almost zero percent, as they have been for almost seven years. Fed Chairman Janet Yellen's explanation for the postponement was riddled with lies. Yellen claimed her decision was based on "strong head winds

United Nations/Faulo Filgueiras

The Hall of the United Nations General Assembly, where the 2015 General Debate will begin with speeches by heads of state on September 28. Both Russian President Putin and U.S. President Obama are scheduled to speak that day.

analysts: Even a minimal interest rate increase of 0.25% would have brought down the entire house of cards of the Transatlantic financial system. And this unavoidable consequence has merely been postponed a little, since Wall Street and the European banking system are hopelessly bankrupt.

What is perfidious about the seemingly endless prolonging of this illness is that the de facto policy of zero interest rates—and soon negative rates—eats up savings and pensions, and drives the savings banks into ruin. When it comes to an uncontrolled collapse—possible at any moment—the result would be chaos, with unimaginable strategic consequences.

from abroad"—a synonym for the latest turbulence on the Chinese stock market.

Several economists—from the chief economist of the Bremen State Bank, Folker Hellmeyer, to the governor of the Reserve Bank of India, Raghuram Rajan—immediately pointed out the inconsistency of this argument. While the Fed reduced its estimate of expected growth in the U.S. economy from 3% to 2.1%, the projection for China was only reduced from 7% to 6.9%; thus it was actually the weakness of the U.S. economy that motivated Yellen, not China's, whose real economy is showing steady growth.

While China is developing its western region with the strategy of the New Silk Road, relies on an economy driven by innovation, and invests worldwide in pioneering projects with many countries, the United States has a monetarist balance sheet, determined by the prices of such essential assets as stocks, real estate, bonds, and other investments. Put another way, while the illusion persists that the speculative values on Wall Street can continue to be honored—we are talking about several trillion dollars—when the crash comes, they will all be shown to be nothing but hot air, virtual money.

The real reason for the Fed's decision is being shouted from the rooftops by the Bank for International Settlements, the German daily *Die Welt,* and various

The BRICS Alternative

Fortunately, the alternatives are already at hand. At the upcoming United Nations General Assembly (UNGA) in New York, it will become clear that the offer of the Chinese to the United States and other important nations—to build the New Silk Road together with China and the BRICS nations in a "Win-Win" framework—is the most important political initiative at this time.

In the days leading up to President Xi Jinping's visit to the United States, agreements have already been signed for China to build a high-speed rail line from Los Angeles to Las Vegas. Perhaps it's not the best choice of route, but at least it marks the beginning of cooperation between these two countries in the field of infrastructure. In the run-up to the UNGA the CEOs of the largest, most important corporations of China and the United States are going to meet. The Chinese wire service Xinhua explicitly repeated Xi Jinping's offer to the United States to work together in building the New Silk Road.

President Putin, in his speech at the UN, will invite the international community to join in a coalition against terrorism, which continental Europe has practically already joined by supporting Russian military operations against ISIS in Syria. Leading political figures in Germany, France, and Italy have underscored this strategic pivot in recent days, with expressions to the effect that neither the threat from ISIS, nor the Ukraine crisis, nor the refugee catastrophe can be resolved without Russia. Putin has set in motion a new dynamic—by sending Russian troops to Syria, proposing a private meeting with Obama in the course of the UNGA, and achieving an understanding between Foreign Minister Lavrov and Secretary of State Kerry on military cooperation between Russia and the United States in Syria.

All of these developments are leading in the right direction. Yet it is necessary to eliminate the fundamental causes that are ultimately responsible for both the threatened Transatlantic financial crash and the refugee crisis. These causes lie in the attempt to maintain a "unipolar world"—a diplomatic circumlocution for world empire—subordinated to the rules of a few banks and corporations, and based on maximizing profits for a small financial oligarchy through speculation—at the expense of the common good. The governments of states that refuse to submit to this world empire are swept away through wars based on lies—hence the refugee crisis.

The best hope is to put an end to the casino economy of Wall Street and the City of London through a return to the Glass-Steagall bank separation law in the United States, and then perforce in Europe. In the U.S. House and Senate, identical Glass-Steagall bills have already been introduced that are garnering more and more support. The re-introduction of Glass-Steagall under these conditions is the hottest issue in the U.S. presidential campaign; it is the sole hope for preventing a chaotic collapse in the coming weeks by getting rid of the toxic waste of the banks pre-emptively.

Should this be done, all doors will be open for the United States and the European nations, together with the BRICS states, to put the policy of the New Silk Road for the economic development of Southeast Asia and Africa on the agenda.

Whether the human race—faced with potential extinction in a thermonuclear war, through a self-imposed descent into chaos and through cultural decadence—has the moral fitness to free itself from this old paradigm and to consciously initiate a new era of human history, will be decided in the next weeks and beyond, in Manhattan.

Be active participants in this decision—not casual onlookers!